PATRIOTIC CITIZENSHIP AND SERVICE IN THE FOURTH REPUBLIC OF NIGERIA

PATRIOTIC CITIZENSHIP AND SERVICE IN THE FOURTH REPUBLIC OF NIGERIA

Isaac Benjamin Eboh

Patriotic Citizenship and Service In The Fourth Republic of Nigeria

Copyright © 2024 by Isaac Benjamin Eboh. All rights reserved.

No part of this publication may be reproduced, stored in a retrieval system or transmitted in any way by any means, electronic, mechanical, photocopy, recording or otherwise without the prior permission of the author except as provided by USA copyright law.

The opinions expressed by the author are not necessarily those of URLink Print and Media.

1603 Capitol Ave., Suite 310 Cheyenne, Wyoming USA 82001
1-888-980-6523 | admin@urlinkpublishing.com

URLink Print and Media is committed to excellence in the publishing industry.

Book design copyright © 2024 by URLink Print and Media. All rights reserved.

Published in the United States of America

Library of Congress Control Number: 2024901613
ISBN 978-1-68486-680-9 (Paperback)
ISBN 978-1-68486-682-3 (Digital)

18.01.24

Dedicated to:
General LEO Irabor
(An outstanding Chief of Defence Staff, Nigerian Armed Forces)

Contents

Chapter 1	Patriotism	9
Chapter 2	History Teaching for Patriotic Citizenship in Nigeria	24
Chapter 3	Service	29
Chapter 4	The Importance of Service and Patriotic Citizenship	44
Chapter 5	The Nigerian Armed Forces as Pivot for Patriotic Citizenship	57
Chapter 6	Military Service and the Invaluable Sacrifice to Patriotic Citizenship and Service	111
Chapter 7	Leadership and Vision	119
Chapter 8	The Pursuit for Patriotism Citizenship and a Genuine Democratic Best Practice for Nigeria	130
Chapter 9	The Threat of Electoral Violence to Patriotic Citizenship	145
Chapter 10	Human Resource Management and Post-Traumatic Disorder: An effect on Patriotic Citizenship	160
Chapter 11	The Nigerian Military as Protectors of Democratic Stability and Patriotic Citizenship	175

Chapter

1

Patriotism

Introduction

Patriotism as a concept means different things to different people depending on the angle it is viewed from. It is also necessary to state here that the place of patriotism in citizenship education is very important considering the various challenges and intrigues that surround the periodic controversies that trail statehood. Patriotism means loving your country and being willing to defend it against its enemies whenever there is the need. It is an emotional attachment to a nation by her citizens. It is a bond that is very strong. It is a sense of affection towards one's country, to such a degree that the individual in the society defines himself or herself through his or her country. Patriots establish interest in the welfare and wellbeing of their country, not minding making sacrifices for the sake of the nation state. It is demonstrated with passion and deep affection for the state. To express their commitment to their countries, citizens are ready to sacrifice their lives, if that would contribute to the survival of their motherland.

The word Patriotic means, supporting one's country. In most developed democracies across the globe like the United States of America, Patriotism is very strong and guarded jealously. It is not personalized for selfish interest but for the benefit of all. In Africa, the concept is not clearly understood especially after colonialism as some early leaders choosed to sit and holdtight the offices of their democratic states to their personal and family interest against the will of the people. In terms of the history of Nigeria, there have been a consistent lack of passion for the deep consciousness that binds citizens of a nation. This is obvious as stated by Isaac Benjamin Eboh (2022), "most Nigerians have developed the attitude of 'No love' for the Nigerian Nation." The political and social implication of this, is that we have a country that is already divided along ethnic and religious lines rather than a united front where citizens put the interest of their country first. This became more obvious in the Fourth Republic with lots of agitations on restructuring. Essentially, the conflictual issues within the context of citizenship and patriotism in the Nigerian State has made room for appropriating "ownership" of the Nigerian State (Adejumobi, 2005), rather than a collective citizenship by everyone hinged on a solid foundation of patriotism. In the context of the United States, the citizen holds his/her country with utmost respect and passion. This is at variant with what is obtainable in the Nigerian State. Political divide has made room for more conflicts of secession rather than a united Nigerian State which was the labours of our heroes past.

Suffice to state here that though patriotism is an ideal that may be difficult to attain, in our contemporary world, there are countries whose citizens do not give it a second thought when the need to pay the supreme price for the survival of the state arises. Unfortunately, in Africa, the concept seems to be clouded with many anomalies. Our elite and political leaders, in their quest for political and economic power, frustrate patriotism among citizens when they use ethnicity and religious bigotry to create division among the people.

The controversy over patriotism and citizen education in a specific schooling system may create some assumptions that might not be accepted by some schools of thought and political philosophers'. The term 'Patriot' and 'Patriotism' entered the English language in conjunction with the rise of the nation state as a political notion but there seems to be a closer connection. In feudal society, the tribal kinship relations were extended with hierarchical relations extending beyond those persons known by an individual. It is significant to state here that the vassal owes fealty to the lord which translate to position and person and by extension to the king and so cannot be a patriot as a matter of choice or commitment. However, with the advent of the nation state, the patriot may be called upon to act in the interest of or defend the king and country. This in early statehood became the measure to define patriotism as the king held sovereign powers to subjugate either the vassals conquered territories or the slaves according to his authority.

A citizen of a nation state is without any personal obligation to a current holder of a social position. Philosophical discussions on patriotism and citizenship education may need to take into account some aspects of the context. For instance, whether the society is in a normal or desirable mode or in extraordinary/crisis mode.

Merry defines 'patriotism' as 'a special affinity one has towards her homeland (or adopted homeland) which fosters a deep psychological attachment and pride.' He identifies 'loyal patriotism' as a disposition of uncritical support for current political leadership and its nationalist ambitions and actions. He argues in his postulation that loyal patriotism in schools is untenable as it conflicts with the legitimate aims of schools. It is important to that these aims include epistemological competence in various disciplines, critical thinking skills and capacity for economic self-reliance. He reiterated that the allegiance of the loyal patriot is coerced and promotes an unhealthy of superiority as well as a misunderstanding of national history. For this study, Merry endorses 'critical patriotism.'

Waghid argues that 'commitment to country in a parochial sense as implied in the (South African) pledge of allegiance, is problematic because, if taught it could result to learners becoming patriotic or failing to recognize the value of reasoned debate....'

Robert derides the common definition of patriotism as love for one's country. He argued for a more idiosyncratic use of 'new patriotism' in New Zealand tertiary education policy documents in which New Zealanders are expected to love their country for its natural beauty, its lack of overcrowding, its distinctive location relative to the rest of the world, its tradition of innovativeness and creativity and its culture of risk taking and entrepreneurialism.

Hand and Pearce see patriotism in a different way. They distinguished patriotism from some normative beliefs about nationalism and special obligations to follow nationals. They find it difficult to identify compelling reasons in favour of patriotism or against it and labeled it as a controversial topic for the school curriculum.

Ide stated the distinctive Japanese connection between patriotic education and peace education. She believes and also sees as anti-nationalists those who link patriotism with nationalism of the kind that resulted in war. Thus, she identifies 'patriotism enthusiasts' as those who link patriotism and peace education as a way of advancing Japanese interests without war. This for this study makes a lot of good meaning.

Patriotism is more pronounced in some countries than others. There are enough facts from Asia to Europe to America, and even parts of Africa, that many countries' social, political and economic prosperity came as a result of citizens' unadulterated loyalty and patriotism. In spite of ethnic, linguistic and cultural diversity, citizens of some of these countries would come together, defend the pride, integrity and interest of their countries, irrespective of the social, economic and political status.

Though patriotism is difficult to measure and quantify. It is important to state here that the World Population Review in its Most Patriotic Countries Report for 2022 which is a product of a survey carried out in 2021, shows that 10 countries stood out. In this report, the percentage of citizens who are devoted and loyal to their countries are as follows; Top on the list is the United States (41%), India (35%), Australia (34%), the United Arab Emirates (27%) and Saudi Arabia (25%). Others are Thailand (25%), Philippines (15%), Indonesia (14%), United Kingdom (13%), and Denmark (13%). One may not totally agree with the outcome of the survey, but Nigerians who have visited some of these countries can attest to a high-level of citizens' loyalty, commitment and patriotism towards their countries.

The heroes of Nigeria's independence recognized the significance of patriotism for national cohesion and development, as is obvious in our National Anthem and National Pledge. However, over the years, the application of the principles that are entrenched in the lyrics of the anthem and pledge have dwindled. Through studies at the level of basic and secondary education, and during training for military and paramilitary services, patriotism is inculcated among Nigerians. However, as the years drag by, patriotism hardly plays out in the lives of certain citizens. This has brought the need for a rebirth in the thinking that concerns the Nigerian citizenry.

Citizenship in Nigeria

Citizenship like many variables is a changing concept and notion. Haynes observed the change from British subject to Australian citizen/British subject in 1949 and the further change to Australian citizen/ Australian subject in 1984. The legal status of citizenship in Australia has changes several times and still subject to change at the determination of the State and Commonwealth legislatures. It is important to note here that the common use of the word 'citizen' is also subject to many uncertainties due to the vague basis to which rights and responsibilities are said to be ascribed to the citizen.

Many developed states of the world are very concerned with the ever increasing immigration numbers from developing countries. In Nigeria, especially Lagos, the former capital of Nigeria, this is called 'japa,' meaning moving to a greener pasture. Although so much is said about multiculturalism and globalism, many of the developed states do not seem to be ready to have other countries nationals overstretch their national capacity and capability to sustain her citizens.

Citizenship is seen as the relationship between an individual and a particular nation. In Nigeria, chapter 111 of the 1999 constitution stated the process of acquiring Nigerian citizenship together with the rights as well as the obligations attached. The Nigerian constitution under section (1) mentioned three bases upon which Nigerian citizenship can be obtained. These are as underlisted;

a. Every person born in Nigeria before the date of independence, either of whose parents or any of whose grandparents belongs or belonged to a community indigenous to Nigeria; provided that a person shall not become a citizen of Nigeria by virtue of this section if neither nor any of his grandparents was born in Nigeria.
b. Every person born after the date of independence either of whose parents or any of whose grandparents is a citizen of Nigeria; and
c. Every person born outside Nigeria either of whose parents is a citizen of Nigeria.

The constitution is very clear on the rights and obligations of citizens. Significantly, it is silent on the rights and obligations of indigenes of various ethnic communities in the country. This lengths weight to some anticipated foreseeable tension that might arise between indigenous Nigerian citizens and settler citizen as its common in Lagos and some parts of the country. However, Sections 42, 43 and 44 of the constitution were entrenched in order to protect both the political and economic rights of settlers' communities in the country. Although these sections made ample efforts to douse tension between indigenous Nigerian citizens and settlers' Nigerian citizens, the problems seem to escalate especially as some party loyalists use their thugs to intimidate Nigerian settlers' citizens to vote for their candidates. This played out significantly in the elections of 2023.

To bring more clarity to the tension between indigenous citizens and settlers citizens, the sections further stated:

Section 42

(1) A citizen of Nigeria of a particular community, ethnic group, place of origin, sex, religion or political opinion shall not, by reason only that he is such a person;
   (a) be subjected either expressly by or in the practical application of, any law in force in Nigeria or any executive or administrative action of the government to disabilities or restrictions to which citizens of Nigeria of other communities, ethnic groups, places of origin, sex, religion or political opinions are not made subject;
   (b) be accorded either expressly by, or in the practical application of, any law in force in Nigeria or any such executive or administrative action, any privilege or advantage that is not accorded to citizens of Nigeria of other communities, ethnic groups, places of origin, sex, religious or political opinions.
(2) No citizen of Nigeria shall be subjected to any disabilities or deprivation merely by reason of the circumstances of his birth.
(3) Nothing in subsection (1) of this section shall invalidate any law by reason only that the law imposes restrictions with respect to the appointment of any person to any office under the state as a member of the armed forces of the Federation or member of the Nigerian Police Force or to an office in the service of a body, corporate established directly by any law in force in Nigeria.

World Citizenship

Since the beginning of the 21st Century and the extensive and rapid growth in technology the internet has been the pivot to most modern interactions' in financial activities as well as other world innovations. All these exploits have brought certain concepts in human relations. Individuals, small scale and medium businesses, organizations as well as governments' and multi-national interests have all assumed new ways of interactions. With the advent of Interest of Things (IoT) a lot have changed in the manner to which things are done. Technology eases the rapid exchange of information both locally and internationally. Companies in developing countries and the developed countries are embracing and possessing huge amounts of data spread across immense structured and giant facilities. The geographical and political boundaries of Patriotic Citizenship have also been challenged by those people who proclaim themselves as citizens of the world. This was during the times of the Diogenes, the Cynic who proclaimed themselves as citizens of the world. They reject the obvious distinction of boundaries with a new concept that is difficult for many races to accept since it negates the tenets of culture and traditional values that have been with man since creation. It may be a reflection of a world view in the type that Russell (1995, p 240). Stoic cosmopolitanism relied on universal natural law like what is obtained in modern versions. Stokes (2000, pp 235-9) identifies three categories of transnational citizenship:

1. Multinational: This is a citizen of multiple sovereign states.
2. International: This has to do with a state like Australia that represents itself as a 'good international citizen' tries to integrate its national interests with respect for humanity and with its responsibilities to help maintain world order.
3. Global:
   (i) Outward looking national citizenship
   (ii) Participation in voluntary non-government humanitarian organizations' and movements.

(iii) Action to create global legal and institutional frameworks.

The idea of global citizenship does not make any sense in this study. This is because the intention is not considered sincere. Racists abuse and discriminations are observed in many world issues. Ethnic rivalries and evils are reported on regular basis in the world. Even in the United State of America, many racial evils are carried out normally with only a few of them that are granted justice. The issues of globalization have reached the level where Herbamas (1996, p 515) states that 'State citizenship and world form a continuum at least are already becoming visible.' Roberts believes that the New Zealand 'new patriotic citizen' will be an enthusiastic neo-liberal citizen of a globalized economy committed to enhancing New Zealand's distinctive contribution. Merry is of the view that a world citizenship view results from students being sensitized to difference and being aware of the danger of assuming that beliefs and values are correct because they are familiar. It reiterated that commitments grounded in partiality provide moral foundations from which to deal with others. These are variance with the typical understanding of citizenship. It will be difficult to attain with so many cases of racial discrimination, ethnic hatred among tribes and the land use laws in some climes channeled against settlers.

Citizenship Education for Patriotism and Service

It is often said that education helps to redefine certain ways that people view things giving them a better and broader perspectives. While patriotism and citizenship seems to be both variables that are vague and unambiguous, education helps to foster the thoughts that the person intends to take to put forward his argument on the matter. The terms can be used in different ways and according to the traditions of the people in question. However, education for Patriotic Citizenship will foster the assumption of the state in question towards the aspect of fostering the stand for a united thinking and assumptions towards building a virile state. Education encourages knowledge and the way a particular state is known among the comity of nations. Nation building will surely be continuous among serious countries that have the desire to excel and improve the affairs of their states. This is not the case with some countries in Africa with so much turmoil and disregard for the rights of the citizens. Rather than encourage Patriotic Citizenship, what we have in these African States are NEUTRAL PATRIOTISM.

The essence for any state to grow above poverty is only based on the need to love one's country. That need is not possible when the high brows and those seen with integrity are liars and without an iota of truth in what they say. It is also important to note that sincere service cannot be attained without patriotism. Service to one's country's best is borne out of patriotism. This can only be achieved with citizenship without bias.

Nigeria's citizenship is filled with so much bias and hatred. The lack of that cohesive unity only leads to lots of criminality and injustice in the land. The Fourth Republic has further heightened the democratic catastrophic embarrassment and lack of honour that is seen in the affairs of the nation.

In most countries in Africa, service is for the personal gains. This is why the Nigerian military stands out over the years for a service that is invaluable since independence from colonial role.

The Fourth Republic has seen a stable democracy with so many challenges. They range from poverty, lack of patriotism, ethnicity, hatred, inter-ethnic violence, brain drain, insecurity, and the entry of Boko Haram and Banditry into the soil of the country. Crude Oil theft in the Niger Delta as well as that of precious minerals such as gold, diamond and many others in Northern Nigeria are stolen without exceptions. Everyday, thousands of barrels of crude oil are stolen from the country. This leaves much to be desired.

The best way of promoting citizenship education is through schools and having the history of the country taught right from infancy. Such teachings should include great personalities that have sacrificed for the independence of the country. The patriots should be praised for loving their countries. Their contributions should be in many monuments as relics for their effort in building their countries. Fallen heroes should also be exemplar of patriots. This also includes the active ones in the military too. This is because their duty in defending the state by land, sea and air puts their lives on the line. The military inculcates that discipline that is required to be a patriot and love for one's country.

In the state of Israel and Japan, citizenship education is captured very early in the child. Although there are claims that Exceptionist states like Israel and Japan have some level of authoritarianist tendencies, this cannot be truly so as religion does not stand in the place of patriotism. Alexander (2000, pp 496-7) states that Israel:

By sponsoring schools that are agents of particular ideologies, the state has supported institutions of indoctrination rather than education. In so doing, it has inhibited the creation of a common vision of the good with which all Israelis, secular or religious, Jew or Arabs can identify. Lacking such a common vision, albeit one that encourages considerable diversity, democracy is greatly imperiled.

Challenges of Indigeneship/ Citizenship Crises in Nigeria

Since independence the problems associated with citizenship and indigeneship have been on the increase. There have been violent conflicts in many parts of the country which escalated to multiple deadly reprisals attacks. This does not augur well with Patriotic Citizenship. The February 2000 riots in Kaduna led to the reprisal killings in the South East. Many innocent people lost their lives. Other crises also erupted in Jos with spillover effects in some parts of the south. Innocent people of different tribes other than the ones involved in the crises lost their lives. These crises are more visible in the Fourth Republic due to the enormous political activities and engagements. Pan-regional consciousness is today replaced by the peculiarities such as indigene, native, autochthonous and origin.

According to Human Rights Watch Report (2001), the violence has brought a lot of distrust and lack of unity among the people. While it is easy to find the Ibos in most part of Nigeria, this constant tribal distrust which leads to wanton killings have forced many of them to flee places where they hitherto had a lot of business going well for them.

In addition to this, some states in Nigeria issue certificates of indigenes in order to give the indigenes privileges and opportunities such as scholarships' and employments, thereby denying other tribes within the geo-political zone. This is called catchment areas. These actions destroy or reduces the principles and efforts to accomplish true patriotism. Unlike some developed democracies and other forms of governments in the world with equity and justice for excellence across board, the Federal Government of Nigeria uses indigeneity as the basis for determining Federal Character. This is a policy which provides all opportunities including, employment, scholarships, appointments into important offices, to reflect the diverse tribes and origins. This gives opportunities to those with lower academic standards from educationally disadvantaged states (Alubo, 2006). While this could appear as a way of balancing political equity, it generates a lot of envy and hatred among the minority groups. In today's Nigeria, it is almost not practiced to its full capacity. This was the error that the military tried to erase after the First Republic.

Strategies to Mitigate the Challenges of Indigenship and Citizenship

The tension that arises from the violent conflict caused by the clashes of indigeneship and citizenship makes it difficult for many to live and invest in places other than where they come from. During the recent election of 25 February 2023, many Ibos and non-Ibos were targeted. Properties' belonging to the Ibos spare parts market were razed down by suspected Yoruba youth due to the mass voting for the Labour Party in Lagos. Even the threats by a famous motor park thug did not have the man arrested for threatening to kill the Ibos in Lagos. The projections for success in national integration as well states autonomy will certainly depend on sincere leadership from both the federal and state governments. There can be no true and sincere coexistence where there are internal suspicions between the indigenes and settlers' citizens. This will go a long way to affect the national security of the country. Certainly, the strategies to be employed to alleviate the challenges between the indegeneship and patriotic citizenship crises to our national security emanates from the following:

a. Constitutional Amendment that will lead to the enactment of Resident Rights. This will require that Patriotic Citizenship must entail the benefit of the law that guarantees that a Nigerian citizen who has resided continually for a period of five years in any state of the federation and did perform his civic responsibilities like the payment of taxes should be entitled to all the rights and privileges of the state. Hence, we will be in accord with the practice in most federations and would straighten the provision in the constitution in addition to removing restriction on who can contest elections in different parts of the country. (Ololade and Ikubaje, 2006). And whether twenty, ten or five, what is being advocated and what is considered relevant is that residency rights be incorporated into the constitution of the Federal Republic of Nigeria.

b. In certain climes like the United States, Israel and Japan, the virtues that are symbolic with the state are high in complete reverence. In the context of the United States, the 'melting pot syndrome,' is very strong. This context is of the view that everything that has to do with the United States of America is superior to any other variable that could be in that particular context. If the context is applied to Nigeria, it will not require that the ethnic groups will not give up their religion, culture, language, customs, music etc. Rather, the concept will seek to strengthen and foster national unity as well as an unweaving integration. This is further heightened by the concept of citizenship which has now assumed the concept of Global Citizenship. The concept of Global Citizenship as earlier discussed in this book will diminish and douse the indigenes and settlers' challenges all over the world. In Nigeria it will partially positively enhance growth and strengthen the concept of Citizenship Patriotism.

Good Expression for Patriotism

This study objects to hate speeches which rather than promote the concept of Patriotic Citizenship encourages tension, disorder and violent conflicts. This plays outs strongly during periods of elections causing many to flee from areas of likely security challenges to safe zones.

Waghid raised an issue that is related to the South African Department of Education's (2001) manifesto on Values, Education and Democracy strategy for schools to be a 'space for safe expression.' That avoids risks of causing distress or discomfort and supports, instead, 'responsible expression' through speech and action that contributes to cultivating a democratic form of patriotism. Responsible expression involves teachers and learners acting 'as friends willing to take the risk of speaking their minds through responsible for "safe" speech.' It further reiterates that responsible expression includes taking risks through belligerent action, such as confrontational deliberation intended to find and enact acceptable terms of political coexistence. This study also presupposes that leaders of all spheres, be it religious, political, academic and all work places must promote the ethics of 'oneness' for the betterment of the state. Patriotic Citizenship therefore, will promote peaceful coexistence among people of different religion, political divide, ethnic groups and ideologies.

References

Adejumobi, S. (2005) "Identity, Citizenship and Conflict: The African Experience," in W. Alade Fawole and Charles Ukaje (eds), The Crises of the State an d Regionalism in Africa: Identity, Citizenship and Conflict, Dakar: CODESRIA.

Alexander, H.A. (2000) Education in the Jewish State, Studies in Philosophy and Education, pp 19, 5-6, pp, 491-507.

Aristotle (1962) Nichmachean Ethics, M Ostwald, trans, (Indianapolis, IN B obbs – Merrill).

Carens, J. H. (2006) Fear versus Fairness: Migration, citizenship and transformation of political community, Philosophy of Education 2006 (Urbana, II, Philosophy of Education Society).

Horgan, D. (2000) Educational Citizenship, in W. Hudson and J. Kane (ed) Rethinking Australian Citizenship (Cambridge, University Press), pp 158-173).

Peters, M, Blee, H and Britton, A. (ed) (2008) Global Citizenship Education: Philosophy, theory and pedagogy (Rotterdam, Sense).

Human Right Watch (2001).

Federal Republic of Nigeria (1999). The Constitution of the Federal Republic of Nigeria.

Chapter

2

History Teaching for Patriotic Citizenship in Nigeria

The history of anything be it individual, things or any aspect of humanity including states and how they evolved is very important. The history of Africa is certainly necessary in this discuss. History helps one to know the origin of anything, how mankind and the earth evolved, the inception of man and the different epochs. The place of patriotism in citizenship education is very important as it will help to foster social cohesion. Also, the place of citizenship education in schooling has proven to be of great significance to countries that practiced it. Michael Merry raised some concerns about the tension that may arise between fostering citizenship and social cohesion. Another aspect was considered to be that of authority and autonomy as an aim of education in schooling. While this position is not observed in most studies in Africa, it will help to change certain perceptions about Patriotism Citizenship and reduce ethnic tension.

It will be observed that the national orientation agency did so much in trying to have a holistic approach towards this social cohesion, which in part is very important as it targets the rural areas too. Liberal democracies face several tension which is drawn from their different cultural and social inclinations. However, to educate for patriotism does not seem to bring out the best in our traditional

Patriotic Citizenship as they lack merit in certain perceptions. The genuineness of the system of government that they seem to run lacks merit with some outright open insincerity. This to a great extent affects the Patriotic Citizenship drives.

Ethnic Patriotic Citizenship

In many countries across the world patriotism could not be easily differentiated with nationalism. Ethnic citizenship cannot be truly tied to Patriotism Citizenship if the collective effort of the whole ethnic citizenship across the state is not adequate to have a true liberal democratic state with equity across board within the various ethnic groups as managed by the government. Ethnic suspicion has brought so much bitterness and violent conflicts in Nigeria even before the beginning of the Fourth Republic. Rather than have the wounds of these conflicts healed with time, the political setting seems to have worsened ethnic suspicion. Although the political elites might claim that all is well with no ethnic suspicion and violent conflicts, the people know the truth as it plays out frequently. In the same vein, the dynamics of various ethnic groups within the Nigerian State has made it difficult for true Patriotic Citizenship. Although the federal character system was put in place to douse these suspicions, it was later misused and abused in a liberal democracy where these ethnic groups even in their little units and lineages suspect each other. This was postulated by Albert, et al (1995:2) when he discussed about conflicts within the psycho-social spheres of man. Here, he suggested that man's action and inactions are products of his psychological formation which are endowed by nature and by the products of the environment that he finds himself through the process of nurturing. It is thus, very difficult to achieve Patriotism Citizenship except with a direct vision change like what is obtainable in Rwanda after painful years of genocide. This is different from what is obtainable in the military. It is a total vow to protect the state irrespective of the odds against her. This is putting one's total loyalty to the state. Everything that is done is for the interest of the state.

There should be conscientious zeal to have the state of Nigeria back to that of a sincere and one cohesive force that is without tribal sentiments and suspicions so obviously displayed at the detriment of Patriotic Citizenship.

The Need to Encourage Patriotic Citizenship in Nigeria

Nigeria in the early 70s was the giant of Africa with the state being at the forefront of championing Africa's total liberation from colonial rule. Great men of honour amongst the then political elites and the military fought at several stages to ensure Africa's complete liberation from the shackles of colonialism. Unfortunately, many years after independence, the Nigerian State seems to be retrograding in her status that truly defined her as the giant of Africa. Her democratic strides are not what it should be many years in the Fourth Republic. Nigeria can only find her feet back if she reinvents herself by once again re-establishing trust and faith in a strong Patriotic Citizenship. When the citizens believe in their country, they will thrive as the citizens will help to make or mar the country. On the contrary, when the citizens do not have absolute hope in the state, they will resort to many nefarious acts which includes exploiting the state and her citizens through crimes of all sorts.

The National Youth Service Scheme which was founded in 1975 by General Yakubu Gowon has been a very good effort to cement the unity of the country. It is very good but the systemic structures through which the country has run over the years is bewitched with lots of institutional evils and decay. The effort to promote patriotism in Nigeria must have its root in citizenship training in our schools. While the NYSC scheme is vital for the unity of the country, it lacks that push to achieve so much within a short time. Kaestle (1983) described how a potent ideology Protestantism, republican civil virtues and capitalism combined to win broad appeal among the middle aged white Americans in the mid- 19th century. He reiterated that by the 1880s the school house flag was very active in hundreds of public schools. Many academicians believe that the flag could garvanised that national sentiment by incorporating daily exposure into public schools. He added that the flag will serve as 'an emotional rallying point' (O Leary, 1999, p,177) for America's school children. The question therefore is, why was there this very strong desire for patriotism? The answer is not farfetched.

Like Nigeria, the nation was almost wrecked by the Civil War and much of the enthusiasm for a united American identity was almost gone. There was therefore a strong and urgent need to rekindle the waned lost identity. Thus, concerted efforts were made to reversed the anomaly. By 1890s, several influences were at work to help rekindle patriotism. A very popular national daily known as the Youth's Champion helped to spread the schoolhouse flag movement. It also helped to inspire patriotic sentiments. The efforts made were able to heal the wounds caused the American Civil War gradually the same way it did after the Rwanda's genocide.

Significantly too, school competitions across both the states and geo –political zones could do a lot to foster the spirit of patriotism. The promotion of loyalty in these schools goes beyond a bond of unity. It translates to the expected bond for Patriotic Citizenship. This loyal patriotic approach will go a long way to stimulate and uphold the values that were meant to bind the state leaving no room for ethnic inclination. Expectantly, the bond that is derived from the military inter-tribal marriages has created so much unity between families of different tribes making it difficult to entertain suspicion of any type. This has made it difficult for the state to completely embrace the legacy of ethnic discrimination as professed in some quarters. There are other inter-tribal marriages' which are borne out of the military legacy since independence. Patriotic Citizenship can thus be encouraged through inter-ethnic marital bonds.

References

Albert I. (2001). Inter-ethnic Relations in Nigeria City. Ibadan: IFRA, p 1.

Amended Constitution of the Federal Republic of Nigeria (2011).

Armitage D (1997) "A patriot for whom?" The afterlives of Bolingbroke's Patriot King. J Br Stud 36:397–418

Berkeley BG [1750] 1953 Maxims concerning patriotism. In: Luce AA, Jessop JE (eds) The works of George Berkeley, vol. 6. T. Nelson and Sons, London, p 251–255

Burkey M, Zamalin A (2016) Patriotism, Black Politics and Racial Justice in America. New Polit Sci 38:371–389

Uchendu, O and Herderson, H. (1965). The King in Every Man. Evolution Trends in Onitsha Igbo Society and Culture. New Haven: Yale University Press, pp .40-41.

Kaestle, C (1983). Pillars of the Republic: Common schools and American 1780-1860 (New York, Hill &Wang).

Ofemu Oratokhai "If Children Behave Badly, Who's to Blame?" www.helium.com/.../74542-if-children-behave-badly-whos-to-blame-parents-or-child? Accessed 10 Feb 2011.

O. Leary, C.E (1999). To Die For: The Paradox of American Patriotism, (Princeton, Princeton University Press).

Zembylas, M. & Boler, M (2002). On the Spirit of Patriotism: Challenges of 'a pedagogy of discomfort,' Teachers College Record: 104:5.

Chapter

3

Service

Introduction

In all spheres of human endeavours, the issue of sincere input to national service have always played very significant point. While a lot of people do not seem to bother a whole lot about their service and achievements in exalted positions, the need for accountability is very necessary. Service to one's nation and in any capacity will bring to bear meaning development across board. The service to one's nation cuts across all works of life, the military, police, medical service, law etc. Bade Gboyega (2004:3) stated that the Public Service means service in any Government capacity as a member of staff within National and State Assemblies, the Judicial Service, the Teaching Service, The Public Enterprises and State-owned Companies, Statutory Corporations, Boards and Commissions and members and officers of the Armed Forces, the Police and (others at the Federal level).

In 1975, the regime of Gen Yakubu Gowon established the National Youth Service Corps in Nigeria. The engagement of young Nigerian grandaunts participants in a mandatory one-year national youth service programmme is a potentially important aspects of encouraging national unity in the country. It is also a way of building selfless service and commitment to the Nigerian State. It is important to note that decades after the entrenchment of democracy in the nation, service to the nation has suffered terribly. The conscientious service to the nation has suffered serious setbacks making it difficult for the country to develop as expected. Many of our leaders went through the national youth service, yet it is difficult to imagine if many of the truly served.

Political leaders usually determine the policies in any nation. These leaders prepare the framework for the political, economic and social directions for the country. It is vital for these policies to be properly articulated and implemented for good results. The development achieved in many countries of the world have been due to the ability of their civil service to effectively translate the policies of their political leaders into concrete services. It also has to do with the selfless willingness by its citizens to serve genuinely.

Section 169 of the Constitution of the Federal Republic of Nigeria (1999) has the subtitle "The Public Service of the Federation" and states there under that "There shall be a Civil Service for the Federation." This portends that the civil service is very important for the development of any nation. This book seeks to put up some significant approach for the sincere need to serve.

The inception of the Fourth Republic which is the current democratic dispensation that began in May 1999 saw the state of the Public Service in Nigeria in terms of public image, value system, operational modality, service delivery in disarray. According to Pepple (2008:3). The dark opinion observed was that the Public Service and the Civil Servants in particular were:

- lethargic and slow in official decision and action;
- insensitive to the value of time;
- irregular in attendance at work;
- nepotic;
- wasteful with government resources;

- poorly staffed and corrupt;
- in appropriately supervised and slow to change;
- characterized by breakdown of disciplinary system and code of ethics; and
- unresponsive and discourteous to the public etc.

This study will highlight the need to serve by creating the impetus, the efforts and achievements like that of a selfless institution. Such evidence would encourage many citizens on the need to be patriotic and serve. The study will look at various issues that would lead to sincere service or otherwise. It would cover from the period of the Fourth Republic up to this day.

Conceptual Clarifications: It is important to have the conceptual clarifications of this particular study. These are discussed below. The first will look at the term public service to which one must have served. These include following;

a. The Civil Service: These are the career personnel in the presidency, ministers' offices, Extra – Ministerial Departments, National Assembly and Judiciary.
b. The Armed Forces, the Police, Other security agencies e.g Para-Military Organisations.
c. The Parastatals or Public Enterprise.

Public Service

This is contained in section 277(91) of the constitution of the Federal Republic of Nigeria of 1979 which is presently found in section 169 of the 1999 constitution as regards to civil service. It is important to state here that the country's government bureaucracy is the Public Service. This is because the government at all levels enunciates and implements its policies, programme and projects through the instrumentality of public service. Significantly, most Public Services are service oriented.

Civil Service

The Civil Service is an organ that is created to ensure that policies and programs of any government in power are carried out. Interestingly, the Civil Service at any point in time does not die. It is the engine room of any government of the day as it is very dynamic. The characteristics of the Civil Service are;

a. It is non- partisan.
b. It is made up of experienced workers, men and women with technical know- how to enable it implement government policies successfully.
c. The Civil Service has to be orderly to enhance the smooth running of the government.
d. The Civil Service is indispensable as it carries out its traditional role irrespective the government of the day.
e. It operates under rules that act as a check to its conduct.

Parastatals or Public Enterprise

This the Operational arm of the government ministers that are established to provide services to the populace. Significantly, the scope of the services that they provide are usually very complex to warrant their establishment as separate bodies outside the normal operations of government departments. It is important to state that the law setting them up does not only allow substantial flexibility as against the rigid demands of Civil Service for high degree of accountability, but also guarantee some level of autonomy. However, the autonomy is subject to the government discretion of their operations to ensure the achievement of important objectives with accountability.

Other Variables and Conceptual Clarifications

Other aspects that are of importance for clarity would be used in this book. These are for the detailed understanding of the various topic that would be discussed. They are; Serve, Code of Conduct, Patriotism, Youth, Poverty, Unemployment, National Security, Leadership, Corruption and Stewardship.

Serve

The word 'serve' is usually associated with works of loyalty and achievements that one carries out in sincerity for one's country. However, let us look at the various meanings of serve. According to the Oxford English Dictionary, the word 'serve' means, 1. Perform or provide service for; be employed (in the Army etc.) 2. Be suitable (for). 3 Present (food etc.) for others to consume. 4. Attend to (customers) 5. Set the ball in play at tennis etc. 6 Deliver (a legal writ etc.) to (a person).

However, for this study, the first meaning would be adopted. This is because it suits what this book tried to portray. The service with regards to what a soldier does for his country is invaluable and a sacrifice. No one can pay for life when it is lost. So also are services that are selfless like that of our founding fathers, Nnamdi Azikiwe who was also knows as the Zik of Africa, the Saudauna of Sokoto, Chief Obafemi Awolowo, Chief Michael Opara, Tafawa Balewa who was the first Prime Minister to mention but a few of them. The selfless service of Alhaji Shehu Shagari who did not have a house after being the President of the Federal Republic of Nigeria, Nelson Mandela of South Africa and a few others represent what this book means by offering that invaluable legacy for others to emulate. It cuts across all works of life including the private sector in impacting on the citizenry.

Youth and Patriotic Citizenship

Africa has the capacity to grow in all areas of human development. There are over 200 million people in Africa who are between 15 and 24 years of age. As the years pass by, the figures increase. The Secretary-General of the United Nations first referred to the current definition of youth in 1981 in his report to the General Assembly on International Youth Year (A/36/215, para. 8 of the annex) and endorsed it in ensuing reports (A/40/256, para. 19 of the annex). Significantly, in both reports, the Secretary-General also recognized that, apart from that statistical definition, the meaning of the term 'youth' varies from one clime to the other. However, the youthful period could be seen as a period of transition from the dependence of childhood to adulthood's independence. It is particularly in relation to education and employment, between the ages of leaving compulsory education, and finding their first job.

The United Nations, for statistical purposes, defines 'youth', as those persons between the ages of 15 and 24 years, without bias to other definitions by Member States. Categorically, this is a period that is very fluid unlike the other groups in the age bracket.

Poverty and Patriotic Citizenship

In Africa, poverty does not represent the divine will of God to mankind. It is rather a place of suffering from childhood to adulthood and death. Sometimes, it is of pain and hardship caused by either natural causes or man. Poverty is a condition where people's basic needs for food, clothing, and shelter are not being met.

According to Aina, poverty is a situation of lack of resources and materials necessary for living within a minimum standard conducive to human dignity and well-being. Unfortunately, this definition is limited in its understanding of poverty by relating it to a minimum standard of living. It does not state what constitutes the minimum standard of living. This definition is therefore, not apt for this study. Daries also defines poverty as a situation where the resources of individuals or families are inadequate to provide a socially acceptable standard of living. However, what is socially acceptable obviously would vary according to class, culture, historical context and power relation. This definition is very contextual and therefore not suitable for this book.

For (Eboh,2022) poverty is a state of complete lack in human necessities that affects the physical and mental well-being of an individual as well as human dignity. This is all encompassing and can be used in this book.

It is important to note that Poverty is generally of two types. There is the 'Absolute poverty' and the 'Relative Poverty.' The latter is synonymous with destitution and occurs when people cannot obtain adequate resources measured in terms of calories or nutrition to support a minimum level of physical health. Absolute poverty is everywhere in the world. However, it is more dominant in Africa. While efforts are being made to eradicate it in other continents, that of Africa seems to be worsening. Even the Millennium Development Goals did not seem to have much impact in Africa.

Let us look at Relative Poverty. This occurs when people do not enjoy a certain minimum level of living standards that could see them through expected problem solving little expectations. It is mostly determined by the government of the day and suffered by the bulk of the population. For example, the deregulation of petroleum products would cause serious hardship to the people. This will automatically cause the rise in transport fares, food items and other sectors of the macro economy. Relative poverty could vary from country to country and sometimes within the same country. Relative poverty may never be eradicated by countries where there is no commodity board price control mechanism as well as countries with very high corruption rate. It is very difficult to have citizens to imbibe true Patriotic Citizenship when they are poor and hungry.

Unemployment and Patriotic Citizenship

Nigeria though a country with enormous human and natural resources has over the years been beset with very high unemployment rate of her teeming population especially the youth. Let us look at what the term unemployment means. Unemployment is defined by the Bureau of Labour Statistics (BLS) as people who do not have a job, have actively looked for work in the past four weeks, and are currently available for work. This also includes people who were temporarily laid off and are waiting to be called back to that job are included in the unemployment statistics. The Covid- 19 pandemic created a colossal damage to the employment of many people across the world as it destroyed many industries as well as small and medium scale enterprises. Unemployment according to Tejvan Pettinger, is a situation where someone of working age is not able to get a job but would like to be in full time employment. This definition is very apt and can be considered for this book.

Security and Patriotic Citizenship

Security is very important for the survival of any state. It is a broad concept that is most often used inadvertently with or without certain considerations of its scope in both intellectual and informal discussions. In the event of an attack on the local population, security may mean to bring solution to the problem by quickly engaging the police, military and other security agencies. It is therefore, important that the crux of this book is the theoretical point of departure of security. Its approach is an all-encompassing perspective. Let us look at each one of them. First is Economic Security which has to do with poverty and unemployment within the state. The second one is Food Security which has to do with the wellbeing and survival of all humans. As earlier stated, when a man is hungry, his Patriotic Citizenship is certainly not existent. Then let us look at the third aspect which is, Health Security. This has to do with the health sector of the state. When the citizens are sick, they will not bother about the state that cannot take responsibility for good and cheap medical approaches to their health challenges. Then, there is the fourth one, which is Environmental Security. It is important to note here that environmental degradation has killed many in Nigeria especially during flood. Pollution in the Niger Delta is a big challenge. There are others that pose a huge threat to human life. The is fifth is Personal Security. This has to do with physical violence, domestic violence, sexual violence as well as child abuse. This is common in poverty ridden areas and places with little or no government presence. Let us look at the sixth one which is Community Security. This is very common especially during election seasons. It has to do with the broad based ethnic and religious intolerance and violence. Inter-ethnic clashes which most often leads to the destruction of lives and properties. The Fulani and Farmers clashes are obvious examples. Then on the final point on the list is the seventh. It is Political Security. This involves human right abuses, political repression, protests over certain political challenges etc. Significantly, the seven variables could affect National Security negatively if not well managed.

In another vein, Security may be considered as assured freedom from poverty or want, precautions taken to ensure against theft, espionage or a person or thing that secures or guarantees (Collins English Dictionary and Thesaurus, 1992). According to Fischer and Green, 'security implies a stable, relatively predictable environment in which an individual or group may pursue its ends without disruption or harm and without fear of such disturbance or injury' (2004, p. 21).

Then let us look at the aspect of traditional definition of security. This may be the provision of private services in the protection of people, information and assets for individual safety or community wellness (Craighead, 2003). In addition, private or commercial security may be considered as the provision of paid services in preventing undesirable, unauthorized or detrimental loss to an organization' s assets (Post and Kingsbury, 1991).

However, security may be expanded to consider national security and the defence of a nation, through armed force or the use of force to control a state's citizens. Security may also imply public policing, with state employed public servants. Additionally, others may consider security as crime prevention, security technology and risk management or loss prevention (Brooks, 2007). Security may be considered as all of these, but this diversity results in a society that has no clear understanding of what security is, with a divergence of interests from many stakeholders (Manunta, 1999). If these aspects are well integrated into the social contract, the people will embrace Patriotic Citizenship.

National Security and Patriotic Citizenship

This is very important for Patriotic Citizenship. Suffice to state here that carrying out excellent services to one's nation owes a lot to her cooperate existence and safety. No nation in the world can boast of a strong foreign policy without her internal and external safety of its people and the defence of her territorial integrity. There is the contemporary concept of national security which places emphasis on physical security. It is worthy of note that before and during the Cold War, the concept of National security was about building up defence and physical security, amassing of weapons and weapon systems. This implied the concerns about secured borders of a nation free from threat of military attack and occupation. All of these have changed as human security is now the basis for national security.

Theoretical Framework on Human Security

Patriotic Citizenship further reiterates as regards the theoretical framework of this study that, we scrutinize the fact that internal security is aimed at ensuring the safety citizens and foreigners as they relate with factors that interact directly or indirectly with them. The United Nations Commission on Human Security (2003) argued for a new aspect of security which is associated with two sets of dynamics. These are:

a. This discourse is of the view that human security is needed to response to the complexities and interrelatedness of both the old and new security threats. This is further related that it is from the chronic and persistent poverty, hunger famine to ethnic, terrorism and religious violence, health challenges like the various variant of Covid 19, and sudden world economic collapse as well as financial instability.
b. Secondly, human security is now seen as a comprehensive approach that embraces all the variables discussed earlier. Thus, human security threats cannot be tackled only through conventional mechanisms but through a new consensus that supports the connections between development, human rights and national security.

Corruption and Patriotic Citizenship

Like some countries across the globe, corruption has been one of the main challenges of the Nigerian State. It has seriously hindered Patriotic Citizenship and Service to the country. It has brought many unpleasant consequences which has given birth to criminal circumstances such as Terror, Advance Fee Fraudsters' also known as '419,' kidnapping and banditry merchants with dare devil security criminals who parade the ungoverned spaces of the country to commit crimes. According to Segun Osoba, corruption is a global phenomenon, intelligible only in its social context. It can he defined as anti-social behaviour conferring improper benefits contrary to legal and moral norms, and which undermines the authorities' capacity to secure the welfare of all citizens.

Many years after colonialism, political life especially in Africa has become dominated by winner-take-all, factional struggles, political cynicism and violence, while the economy and social institutions have been driven into decay. This cannot encourage Patriotic Citizenship in its real sense of it. Corruption has thus become a way of life in many African countries making most of its state lacking the ability to sustain a standard life for majority of her citizens. Combating corruption requires a popular participatory democracy able to monitor and hold to account those in charge of the state and the treasury. What has happened in Nigeria lately where the head of the Central Bank was arrested with so many allegations only shows that corruption almost destroyed the country's economy.

Without doubt, Nigeria has consistently been known for her corrupt ranking in the world corruption index. According to Transparency International Corruption Perception Index 2011, Nigeria ranked 143 out of 183 countries across the world. The record does not witness any level of improvement but it gets worse by the day. Corruption has eaten deep into the fabric of the Nigeria State making it fashionable in many parlances. Significantly, this has given rise to many crime merchants who sponsor various dynamics in the nation's security threat such as terrorism, kidnapping and various evils across the unmanned spaces of the country. Political rivalries motivate the growth of acts of terrorism in any country. The level of corruption embedded in a political system makes it easy for terrorism and ethnic militias to carry out their operations with impunity.

Additionally, corrupt political elites in an attempt to take back power from the ruling political party encourage criminal activities which encourage illicit trade in hard drugs, illegal small arms proliferation, illegal migrations, oil bunkering, oil theft, budget padding, treasury lootings to mention but a few. These politically induced crimes have been more prevalent in Nigeria after the Fourth Republic took over power in 1999. This for this study has encouraged a lot of anti patriotic challenges. There is the need for such trends to be aborted.

Nation- building/ Nationhood

This study wishes to clarify that Nations are otherwise also referred to as States. They are the basic unit of man's political organisation. Significantly, every country in the world is concerned about the improvement of the living standards of its citizens. Thus, there are nations that strive well by giving the citizens the benefit of serving their countries well. There are also nations with leaders that do not seem to care. With such nations the citizens seek for dual or more citizenship as they do not feel fulfilled with their original countries. Efforts should be made by African States to discourage such trends as it leads to exodus movement with the resultant effect of brain drain in many African States.

Significantly, Nation-building is the coming together of different ethnic groups to form a political entity known as a country. It is a conscious attempt by some nationalists to form a political unity in the form of a state. This process according to Halima (2010), aims at the unification of the people within the state that remains politically stable and viable in the long run. Nations are built by people with vision and self-determination like the founding fathers of Nigeria. It is therefore, the product of a conscious statecraft effort through political meetings and agreements towards development, co-existence, tolerance and economic growth. Kabir and Mustapha (2010) added that nation building is "a deliberate attempt to bring together all components parts of a geo – political entity for oneness of purpose in growth and development." Therefore, the term nation building stands out everytime and everyday. It is ageless and without limit. This invariably bring us to the question:

> "Have you truly served your country, or you brought pain to her citizens?"

The answer could be from the consciousness of one's personal judgement if that political office holder in whatever capacity made that government appointment better than he met it or if he simply made enormous personal gains from it leaving the place decayed.

Theories used for Study

Certain theories were used to buttress important facts and place them on the context to which academic discourse could be determined. One of them is based on the Feierabend and Betty Nesvold theory (1969) known as Raising Expectation Theory. When states are created through political machinery and agreements, much is expected from the union of different tribes and religious background to coexist as one body to form a united front for the benefit of all the component parts of that union. The Unites States of America falls into this theory with many races forming a strong and viable country. Another theory used in this book is that of Robert Gurr et. Al (1971: 569-604) known as the Relative Deprivation Theory. It is important to state here that both Raising Expectation Theory and the Relative Deprivation Theory are said to be the twigs from Frustration – Aggression Theory. This was originally said to have been postulated by John Dollard et al (1939). According to Dollard et al, "the occurrence of aggressive behavior always presupposes the existence of frustration and that the existence of frustration leads to some forms of aggression." This is further reiterated that aggression is caused by frustration which is as a result of certain denials. Gurr in his deprivation thesis argued that the potential for any collective violence especially the one that spanned over time is a function of the intensity and extent of shared dissatisfactions among members of the society. He added that the incentives for political violence is a function of the degree to which such shared dissatisfactions are blamed on the political system and its agents. This does not encourage Patriotic Citizenship. It is seen as a chaotic state where anything goes. The state is not respected and her citizens are not honoured except for those with the values of the countries where they sojourn.

Conclusion

The zeal and patriotism to serve one's nation determines the collective attitude to which the nation's growth is determined. Such sacrifices make room for conscious effort by the citizenry to emulate the attributes that they see in their leaders at all levels. The dynamics that exist between political groups and the contextual situations of personal driven virtues leads to anger and frustration which such actors further gear towards a negative reprisal to the state in form of politically motivated crimes rather than service to a nation that they milked with their callous greed. Political uncertainty makes the citizens to moan the defects and hardship that they face. This chapter is axle to other issues that would be discussed.

References

A Daries, Poverty in Third World Countries, (London: Taristock, 1999).

Ake, C. (2000). The Feasibility of Democratisation in Africa: Darka CODESRIA.

Conte – Morgan, E. (1977). Democratisation in Africa: The Theory and Dynamics of Politics.

Danjuma, T.Y. (2002). The Difficulties and Deficiencies of our National Security. A need for control measures for National Security. A paper presented at the senate security conference in Abuja – Nigeria.

Eboh, I.I.B. (2022). The Frightful Patriotism and Peace Resolutions in the Fourth Republic of Nigeria.

Nnoli, O. (1978). Ethnic Politics in Nigeria. Enugu Fourth Dimension Publishing Company.

O Mbachu and C Mayor, (eds) Democracy and National Security: Issues, Challenges and Prospects, (Kaduna: jake Graphic Printers, 2009).

UN Poverty Development in Africa Social and Economic Policy at <http://www.globalpolicy.org>, (20 Oct 10).

Chapter

4

The Importance of Service and Patriotic Citizenship

Introduction

Service is one of the most important indices to the development of any state. Where there is honesty and diligence in the discharge of duties, one is bound to see adequate rise in the standard of living of the people. In the early 60s shortly after independence Nigeria was highly respected because she had leaders of high repute who put their country first.

Nigeria had different industries that helped to boast her economy in textiles, vehicle assemblies, cash crops cultivation and exportation such as cocoa, cotton, rubber, hides and skin and many local industries with significant levels of exportations. This was shortly before oil was discovered. The growth of nations has to do with quality of service. This has to be in all sectors of the economy as well as the civil service. Rather than treat these issues with kid gloves, effort must be made to sincerely address them.

On the educational sector, there seems to be a drastic decline when compared to the quality education of the past. The decision the Federal Government of Nigeria to introduce the Universal Basic

Education (UBE) programme necessitated the Nigerian Educational Research and Development Council (NERD) to restructure and re-align the curricular into a 9-year Basic Education was premised on the attainment of Education for All (EFA) Goals, National Economic Empowerment and Development Strategies (NEEDS) and the Millennium Development Goals (MDGs). However, the question is if these efforts have been translated to actual success is what seems to affect what a true service should be. Unfortunately, our educational challenges seem to be getting worse by the day as politicians bask in the euphoria of plenty while the academic sector wallow in degradation and strikes. This is not good for the growth of any nation as it affects both the micro and macro aspects of the economy. The ecosystem of this economic chain has left many back into abject poverty.

Service to our nation at this moment of the country's history is very important. This is because we must endeavour to put the country first. The nation is faced with many challenges which are caused by our lack of interest or back stand on the nucleus of nationhood that should bind us together as a nation. Our service to the nation is today not yielding the desired results. People are no longer citizens driven making service a mockery of itself. Today, most of the private and public sectors of our economy giants' industries and companies have either gone into bankruptcy or are operating at lower capacities. The exchange rate is exorbitantly outrageous caused by our inability to export so as to earn foreign exchange.

The post coronavirus era added to the nightmare of the problems increasing further the crime rate in the Nigerian State. Although many people died in the heat of the pandemic, the question about service readily comes to mind on the dilapidating state of our hospitals. Not many people especially the poor can afford many of the medical services. The medical sector that should rather have a sound and vibrant part of the wellbeing of our citizens is rather seen to be consultation points, with lots of collapses in physical service rendering. Most of the care givers behave as though they are doing favours to the helpless patients who sometimes have nowhere else to go. Many of them resign to fate and die due to these poor service. The fact is that poor service is inimical to the growth and development of the economy of any nation. It should be a good source for Patriotic Citizenship.

Many Nigerians tend to relocate abroad to seek for greener pastures where they assume they could be better paid for their services. The challenges of the Nigerian State today call for the question of service that we render to our country at all levels. For a country that is presently pestered with ethnicity, religious, political and security challenges, it becomes very necessary for all to wake up to the responsibility of saving our country from total collapse.

With the institutional decay of the various sectors of the Nigerian State, there is the need to add other variables to this discourse. This is that democracy and social justice should be fundamental precondition for peace, security and conflict management. While the military has done so much to ensure that the Nigerian State is safe and secured, it is important to state here that development and peace will be elusive under conditions of unhealthy unresolved democratic challenges. In an environment with deficient public service delivery, the need to take stock and reassess the problems being faced makes this study very necessary and important.

A lot of scholars have attempted to use dynamics to explain the conditions that prevail in the country considering it as a near collapse challenge which affects the common citizenry. There used to be a time when civil service worked in Nigeria. There was a time when Nigerians could travel from the nooks and crannies of this great nation unhurt. While a lot of people blame our situation to the unpatriotic democratic practice by our political elites, the question about service still comes to mind.

Legacy of Service as evidence of Patriotic Citizenship

Service to one's nation is very important. Where people are not committed to the service of their nation, the best can certainly not be achieved. In the early 70s, most things that had to do with service were done with honesty. A taxi man will render his service conscientiously without exploiting his clients. A shoe mender will not do a bad job and expect to be paid. A mechanic will provide service that is acceptable. The list goes on and on from the micro to the macro economy. Additionally, many distinguished persons like Professor Wole Soyinka, Professor Chinua Achebe, Chief Obafemi Awolowo, Gani Fawemi, Dr Nnamdi Azikiwe, Sadauna of Sokoto, Maitama Sule (the orator) Sir Abubakar Tafawa Balewa to mention but a few of them were seen by the youth at that time and young Nigerians as their mentors. It was easy to see kids desiring to be doctors, lawyers, literary icons, architects, engineers and our adorable military. It was a great pride to be a soldier of the land, sea or air sphere of the military.

So, the joy of patriotism was the quality service that we enjoyed irrespective of tribe and religion. General Yakubu Gowon brought unity to the nation after the Civil War. His name carried the acronym; Go On With One Nigeria. General Murtala/Obasanjo's government helped to liberate some African States from apartheid and colonialism. There were many who did not enrich the state on the account of their exalted positions. This was service without blemish. True leaders do not use power to empower themselves. Service is the greatest art of leadership. It was very rare to see conflict translate into a full blown violent conflict after the Nigerian Civil War. The nation was filled with citizens who considered their services very important for nation building. Nigeria had the potential to feed her citizens and still offered diplomatic assistance to other nations.

Nigeria Civil Service was one of the best in the world due to its honesty and due process regulations which was revitalized during President Olusegun Obasanjo's government. Nigeria was a great country that offered financial relief to many African States such as South Africa, Botswana, Zimbabwe, Angola, Chad, Niger Republic etc. Her citizens were respected and loved. The joy of every village or town was to have a son or daughter of their soil who had truly served his country well not looters of government funds and not those who were regarded as bad eggs of the country.

Quota System in the Nigerian Federation as Encouragement for Patriotic Citizenship

This is otherwise known as the federal character principle. It came with the presidential system of government which also came with the 1979 constitution. It was modelled after the United States of America system of government. It is important to note that Nigeria before then had the parliamentary system of government. This present system was adopted to embrace the diversity of the Nigerian State without enmity, religion and the cultural divide in all spheres of her political realities.

The importance of this was to balance the appointments, selections to various Federal Government establishments like unitary schools, sectors with the federal holdings, public service, the military, health police, aviation, other security agencies etc. The principles of the federal character as propounded by the military government then sought to douse tensions of ethnic dominance in key appointments as well as other opportunities in the Nigerian State. This was to avoid conflicts and suspicion. The qualified citizens were to be picked based on excellence and without bias. However, over time, the Quota system began to experience cracks as politicians and democratic elites put the honesty of the system to test and challenges. This did not support Patriotic Citizenship and Service.

Code of Conduct for Patriotic Citizenship

It is very important to look at the meaning of the above concept as we delve further into this study. Thus, Code of Conduct is a set of rules, regulations, expected responsibilities, proper practices for an organization, party, union or a group of people working together to achieve certain goals. This could be seen as ethics, honour, values, moral codes as well as some level of religious uprightness. It could also be seen as, principles, standards, rules of behavior that guide the procedures and systems of an organization in a way that it positively affects the rights of all the constituents affected by its operations. For the civil service, these rules are there and must be observed irrespective of the government of the day. It is the engine room for good and efficient performance based on sincerity and the ethics that are expected from time to time.

The Code of Conduct for Public Officers to Enhance Patriotic Citizenship

In most countries of the world public officers in particular are expected to have a high sense of honesty and integrity. It is important to also adduce here that public service is the machinery that the government uses to render service to its people. Quality public service will holistically affect the standard of living of the citizens within the shores of that country. For example, a drop in the standard of education in the country will mean that its public servants from the Minister of Education, Permanent Secretary and many key workers have failed in their responsibilities to render quality service to the people. In countries like the United States of America, China and Japan, such key appointees should resign voluntarily. This also applies to other sectors. Unfortunately, in Nigeria people behave the way they like as though there are not sets of rules that govern our conduct.

The process of rendering public service must conform with proscribe code of conduct provided by the constitution. It is therefore, important to state here that the process of carrying out service has been spelt out in the constitution of the Federal Republic of Nigeria. It guides public servants in the way they should discharge their duties. It is on record that the former Prime Minister of Great Britain Boris, resigned his appointment on the grounds that he bridged the public service code of conduct.

Let us look at the code of conduct as enshrined in the Nigerian Constitution. Essentially, the 1999 constitution, part 1 of the fifth schedule clearly made adequate provision for the work attitude of public servants or public office holders. It further reiterates that public servants must be held responsible on account of their wrong attitude to work. Thus, section one provides that a public officer should not put himself in a position where his interest conflicts with his duties and responsibilities. This will be examined as we proceed with this views. Have we truly served our nation? Were the public service norms not the same as in terms of integrity before and after we progressed further in 1999? Section 1 as earlier stated, has to do with the common law duty to act in good faith. Thus the law imposes on the officer to act in good faith in situations where his personal interest clashes with his duties and responsibilities as a public servant. The rule is strict and requires that public officers should not allow themselves to fall into such a dilemma as the law will definitely catch up with them.

Significantly too, section 2 (a) states that a public officer should not receive or be paid emoluments of any public office at the same time he must not receive or paid the emolument of any other public officer. This rule invariable states conflict of interest as implied in the first rule. It restricts public officers being paid emolument from two different offices. This is very interesting as it particularly brings to mind the Academic Staff Union of Universities (ASUU) strike which lingered for more than six months. It brings much to be desired as the complexities of demands not only from the Academic Staff Union of Universities but from other groups that came up with their demands. Government is not likely able to handle the financial implications. However, as we make progress on this study, there is the need for us to look at The Treasury Single Account;

Treasury Single Account

This is a public accounting system that should have long been operational during the government of former President GoodLuck Ebele Jonathan. It was designed to cut the excesses of many aspects of governance especially for many who get paid by government more than once. The purpose is to manage the government revenue and ensure that the payments comes through the Consolidated Revenue Account (CRA) of the Central Bank of Nigeria. Significantly, it was introduced in 2012 as a trial project and began its operation in 2015. It covers all of the existing Ministries, Departments and Agencies (MDAs). However, companies in the oil and gas industry, as well as other joint venture partners' accounts, are excluded from the Treasury Single Account's responsibilities.

Advantage

a. Battle Corruption.
b. Make sure government payments are transparent.
c. Allowed FG to discover and close 17, 000 Accounts in Commercial Banks with 0 interest rates.
d. Discovered and shut down some fake Accounts operated by private establishments which did not benefit government.
e. Helped Nigeria to get better hold of its finances.
f. Bankers and civil servants are no longer able to get 10 percent interest on government funds.
g. The money that belongs to the government is under its full control than ever.
h. More online banking features and more payment opportunities.
i. Able to monitor government profits and transactions.

Disadvantage

This system has its challenges. The first was that;

a. Anything new is always difficult.
b. Many autonomous institutions might lose their operational independence.

This study will also look at another similar system which the Federal Government used to cut down lots of excesses. This one is known as the Integrated Personnel and payroll Management System;

Integrated Personnel and Payroll Management System

Like the Treasury Single Account, the Integrated Payroll and Personnel Information System (IPPIS) is an information Communications Technology (ICT) project initiated by the Federal Government of Nigeria (FGN). Significantly, the Aim is to improve the effectiveness and efficiency of payroll administration for its Ministries, Departments and Agencies (MDAs). This is in line with the anti-graft stance of the present administration. The Federal Government has directed Ministries, Departments and Agencies (MDAs) to migrate to the Integrated Personnel Payroll Information System (IPPIS) to check perennial wastes and leakages in government. This is also where the Academic Staff Union of Universities (ASSU) is refusing to accept like the first system stated in this book. Let us look at the points underlisted;

a. In the Armed Forces, the Nigerian Army complied by first quarter of 2018 in spite of its obvious peculiarities. Other services followed in the second quarter.
b. Special features examines the effects of ghost workers' syndrome and how the implementation of the IPPIS could address the menace in the Armed Forces in particular, and public service in general.

c. The ghost worker syndrome has taken a dangerous dimension in Nigeria, with government spending billions of naira year-in-year-out resulting from the money being siphoned through fictitious payments.
d. Consequently, the geometric annual increase in wage bill has become worrisome with the attendant economic consequences.
e. A Nigerian minister of finance in February, 2011 revealed that the pilot implementation of the integrated personnel and payroll information system (IPPIS) in sixteen ministries, departments and agencies (MDAs) saved the nation over N12 billion between 2007 and 2010 respectively.
f. The pilot implementation was necessitated by the fact that government wage bill had constituted a huge chunk of recurrent expenditure, up to 58 percent of the annual budget.
g. In 2014, Ngozi Okonjo Iweala observed that as part of measures aimed at cushioning the effect of dwindling oil revenue, government saved 160 billion naira by weeding out 60,000 ghost workers from the payroll.
h. This is also excluding the 46,821 ghost workers identified in 215 ministries, department and agencies in 2013.
i. Hence, the consistent staff screening in government ministries, departments, agencies both at the federal, states and local governments is the manifestation of the level of ghost workers' syndrome in the public service.

The staff audit exercise conducted in federal capital territory in 2013 revealed that out of 26,017 on the payroll, 6000 were fictitious. The audit exercise further exposed the extent of monumental corruption, theft and financial irregularities associated with the old system.

j. In compliance with Federal Government directive to Ministries, Departments and Agencies (MDAs) to migrate to the Integrated Personnel Payroll Information System (IPPIS) in the wake of introduction of the Treasury Single Account (TSA), the Minister of Finance represented by the Secretary, Presidential Committee on Continuous Audit, said that when fully implemented, the scheme would ensure prompt payment of salaries and allowances and checkmate diversion of funds meant for troops to other purposes.

k. He said the Treasury Single Account (TSA) and the IPPIS are aimed at improving accountability and optimizing Government payroll system.

Having looked at these two systems, it can be deduced that the efforts of the government to cut down all these loop holes that so many unpatriotic citizens have benefitted from is a step worth taking. The fight by the university lecturers and academia and its numerous demand does not show any realism of achievement. The question is, does it negate the code of conduct? Is it Patriotic Citizenship compliance?

Emolument

Let us look at the meaning of emolument. According to the section 19 of the Fifth Schedule of the 1999 constitution, emolument means;

> "Any salary, wage, over time – or lave pay, commission, fee, bonus, gratuity, benefit, advantage (whether or not that advantage is capable of being turned into money or money's worth), allowances, pension or annuity paid, given or granted in respect of any employment or office."

Additionally, sub paragraph (b) of this section, restricts public officers from engaging or participating in the management of running any private business, profession or trade except where his employment is on part- time basis. However, this rule did not prevent public officers from engaging in farming. There are several other sub paragraphs with different rules. However, this study will limit itself only to the ones earlier stated above.

Establishment of Code of Conduct of Bureau and Tribunal

In 1988, the Political Bureau recommended to the Federal Government the need to strengthen the existing machineries for monitoring the actions and behaviours of public officers to ensure that they do not fault in morality and accountability. This was because the Bureau observed that indiscipline and corruption were the main challenge to our development. Thus, the recommendations of the Bureau led to the establishment of the Code of Conduct Bureau and Code of Conduct Tribunal. This has been able to monitor the conduct of public officers to avert abuse of office. For example, it made it compulsory for certain categories of public servants to declare their their assets before assuming certain exalted positions.

Conclusion

The Public service is very significant in the running of any government. It is the hub for public service delivery and governance. The quality of public service delivery will go a long way to determine the development of the state. A good public service will not have the enormous indiscipline and corrupt practices as presently experienced by the Nigerian State. Ghost workers have been a thriving business and the high toll of theft by exalted public office holders who should rather be made to cool their feet in prison than walk tall in the society.

The public officers who are meant to propel the engine of state development must be seen above board in their conduct as examples to their subordinates. This is because of the sensitivity of the policies and programmes that they formulate. They must be very reasonable to the common man and should therefore function properly. The constitution of Nigeria has therefore, enshrined the expectations and sanctions for erring public servants.

This study is of the view that public servants who ruin the attitude to serve sincerely should be sanctioned appropriately without bias. Therefore, the need for service should be the watchword of every citizen. The question is therefore, have you truly served your country? Is the service you render Patriotic Citizenship biased or for personal gain?

References

Adebo A. Why Code of Conduct Bureau should not be removed from the constitution (2012) available at www. Thislive.com/article/why-code-of-conduct-should not-be removed- from-the-constitution. Access on 05/02/2015.

Carl, L. (2005). Federal Structures, Decentralization and Government Performance in Nigeria, In Onwudiwe E. and Suberu R. t. (eds) Nigeria Federalism in Crisis, a Critical Perspective and Political Options, PEFS; University of Ibadan.

FRN (2011) The 1999 Constitution of the Federal Republic of Nigeria with amendments 2011.

O.F Ayodele, 'Performance Measurement and Management', a publication of the National Open University, school of Business and Human Resources Management, Lagos <www.nou.ng? Accessed on 20/06/2014.

Chapter

5

The Nigerian Armed Forces as Pivot for Patriotic Citizenship

Introduction

The Nigerian Armed Forces which is the main strong point in the issues regarding Patriotic Citizenship is seen in this study as that cohesive force that keeps the nation state together amid her many troubles and challenges. The Nigerian State has a very strong military which contributed immensely to the peaceful settlement of violent conflicts across the world especially within the West African Region. Nigeria chairs the operations of the Economic Community of West African States (ECOWAS). Nigeria has in the past contributed its troops for peace keeping operations within the West African sub region, East Africa and Burma during World War 2. This study intends to add that Nigeria funded a bulk of the peace keeping operations and was regarded as the 'Giant of Africa.'

The Fourth Republic which began in 1999 has witnessed a complete stay off by the military from the political landscape of the country to make way for a complete democratization of the Nigerian state. While the political context of this has changed dramatically and hopes for liberalization and particularistic exclusions drastically on the forefront, the military has maintained its total allegiance to its military tenets. The military has taken a back seat, as it returned to the barracks to focused on its constitutional role of defending the country. As earlier mentioned, the military has also carried out external operations, notably the Economic Community of West African States (ECOWAS) Cease-fire Monitoring Group (ECOMOG) in Liberia and Sierra Leone in 1991 and 1997, respectively, as well as being involved in the ECOWAS military intervention in The Gambia in 2017. Its Patriotic Citizenship embracing officers and men have individually or as a group served in several United Nations Peace keeping and Peace Support Operations across the globe. Suffice to state here that some distinguished military officers have served in different capacities in the United Nations missions all over the world. This is a complete testament to the excellence and valour that the Nigerian Armed Forces is known for. It is important to note that the President of Nigeria functions as the Commander-in-Chief of Nigeria's Armed Forces. He gives directives on important and sensitive operations as well as other matters concerning the military and the military veterans.

The Chief of Defence Staf is in control of the Armed Forces of Nigeria. He directs the joint operations and training of the three services/branches that make up the Armed Forces of Nigeria. The Chief of Defence Staff works with his military subordinates who are the three Service Chiefs (Chief of Army Staff, Chief of Naval Staff and Chief of Air Staff). They are responsible for the running of their respective services. For this study, the Systems Theory to aid Patriotism Citizenship is used. It will not emphasize much on Citizenship Education here as the military already has its solidified trainings where this is inculcated on its military citizens. It is this regimental Patriotic Citizenship education and practice that distinguishes them from the Nigerian society.

Systems theory: This is the interdisciplinary study of systems, i.e. cohesive groups of interrelated, interdependent components that can be natural or human-made. Every system has causal boundaries, is influenced by its context, defined by its structure, function and role, and expressed through its relations with other systems. A system is 'more than the sum of its parts' by expressing synergy or emergent behaviour. This for this study, invariably means that the Armed Forces of the Nigerian State is a system that works in an unbroken synergy. The system is controlled by the Chief of Defence Staff who controls the component military force of land troops, naval troops and air troops in a collective reality of Patriotic Citizenship. The military system is very unique as it has a lot to do with honour, competence, trust and the reality on ground. The military systems have to work together to achieve the safety of the sovereignty of Nigeria through land, air and sea. A change in one part of the system could affect the whole. Suffice to state here that some countries in the world only have one military service which is the land component. However, they usually have a small unit of the air fighter crafts attached to the land troops. Example is the Republic of Chad.

The Armed Forces in the Nigerian Constitution

The Armed Forces was not formed out of the blues or by anyone. It is the product of the Nigerian Constitution. This is the same with other institutions in the country. Section 217 of the 1999 constitution (as amended) makes the provision of the Armed Forces of Nigeria legal. It also stipulates the functions and responsibilities of the military.

It states:

217(1) There shall be an armed forces for the Federation which shall consist of an army, a navy, an air force and such other branches of the armed forces of the Federation as may be established by an Act of the National Assembly.

217(2) The Federation shall, subject to an Act of the National Assembly made in that behalf, equip and maintain the armed forces as may be considered adequate and effective for the purpose of –

a. defending Nigeria from external aggression;
b. maintaining its territorial integrity and securing its borders from violation on land, sea, or air;
c. suppressing insurrection and acting in aid of civil authorities to restore order when called upon to do so by the President, but subject to such conditions as may be prescribed by an Act of the National Assembly; and
d. performance such other functions as may be prescribed by an Act of the National Assembly.

Furthermore, Section 218(1), (2) and (3) of the constitution confers the President with the "power to determine the operational use of the armed forces of the Federation", to appoint the Service Chiefs and to delegate functions to any member of the Armed Forces of Nigeria.

Section 5(5) of the constitution also empowers the President to deploy military officers to engage in combat duties outside of the country, but the President must "seek the consent of the Senate and the Senate shall thereafter give or refuse the said consent within 14 days."

The Fourth Republic and the Changing Phase of Security Threats; Terrorism, Banditry and Kidnapping

With the inception of the Fourth Republic in 1999, many Nigerians thought that the best had come the Nigerian democratic setting. Many scholars blamed the military for the country's woes that made visible contributions towards nationbuilding and assisted many African countries to regain their independence from colonialism. Today, the situation is worse with ethnic suspicions and threats of insecurity all over the country. Reconciliations through nationbuilding is worsened by democratic injustices. Millions of Nigerians have lost hope in the political gladiators who destroy the hopes of Patriotic Citizenship. The so called forced Nigerianism through national discipline and citizenship which was said to have been placed on the people is today captured by the mirage of political thugs and miscreants. Today, there are rising distrust between the Yorubas and Ibo in Lagos, the Fulanis and the Hausas and many unknown tribal conflicts across the country. Nigeria is slowly dwindling to a degrading state as the once giant of Africa.

The issues of terrorism have kept many countries on their toes. In Nigeria, this suddenly, as in other parts of the country like with the Maitasine group tried to get dominance. Unfortunately for them, the military in its zero tolerance to this, flushed them out completely. The entry of the Boko Haram insurgency into the Nigerian soil was shortly after the death of President Alhaji Musa Yar Adua. He was for this study an embodiment of Patriotic Citizenship. He wanted to bring the best to his country. After his death came his Vice President, Dr Goodluck Ebele Jonathan, an amiable and humble Patriot. Like his boss, he wanted the best for the Nigerian State. Unfortunate, too many evils stood on his way. The Boko Haram terrorist group penetrated the country and almost laid siege of the Federal Capital Territory. The Police Headquarters' and the United Nations Headquarters' in the Federal Capital Territory were attacked simultaneously. The Fourth Republic political governance almost distorted the long years of military and police excellence across the globe. This study also wishes to state that the Nigerian Police Force has excelled in many countries in the world especially in Africa. The Force was instrumental to the setting up of many countries Police Forces in Africa during the military regimes. The Force has gotten medals in many United Nations Missions. Although the Nepal Police Force was earlier seen as one of the outstanding, the Nigerian Police Force became a role model to standards of policing in Africa.

The Nigerian Armed Forces and Operational Exploits

The Nigerian Armed Forces has carried out various successful operations across the country and its participation in Peace Support Operations with the United Nations has been commended for their steadfastness and commitment and remaining firm and decisive in upholding the tenet of Patriotic Citizenship as it observed its constitutional roles. The Nigerian Armed Forces has contributed immensely in keeping the nation as one virile entity. The Armed Forces is today having multiple security challenges to handle much more than the period before the Fourth Republic. This is partly because democratic governance in Nigeria is beset with too many challenges many of which are violent conflicts.

The prominence of the Nigerian Armed Forces in the Fourth Republic democracy cannot be overemphasized. In May 2009, the country celebrated ten years of uninterrupted democracy. Beyond her constitutional role, the military is a national asset and a tool for national cohesion. As a matter of fact, the military is the soul of a nation. From its records in peace-keeping missions and other pro-democracy engagements across the world, the Nigerian military could be comfortably referred to as an outstanding and formidable force. A few years ago, a warship was deployed to force out The Gambian dictator, former President Yahya Jammeh.

The Nigerian Armed Forces have effectively suppressed civil disorder and other forms of armed conflicts in the country. Significantly, the military is no longer the nation's last line of defence due to many threats to the security, stability, peace and unity of the country. It is today the first line of defence in the country. This is because the military had never been so engaged in heterogeneous internal security operations as it is now in the history of the nation. This has made the military to significantly expand and increase its strength. The Armed Forces is presently overloaded with the responsibility of engaging serious armed conflicts ranging from insurgency, banditry, kidnapping, armed robbery, cattle rustling, farmers-herdsmen clashes, pipeline vandalism, electricity cable vandalism, oil theft, illegal bunkering, ritual killing, electoral violence, cultism and lots of other terrible crimes. These are all threats to national stability. There is hardly a day that these crimes do not happen in the country amid extreme poverty. These internal crises in many parts of the nation have overwhelmed the civil police. It is therefore, necessary that the military always ensured that emerging internal security threats do not degenerate or escalate to the point of consuming the entire country or any of its federating states.

The Boko Haram insurgency has led to deaths of thousands of people both military and civilians. Two million, one hundred and fourteen thousand (2,114,000) persons have become internally displaced as at December of 2016, with 537,815 in separate camps; 158,201 are at official camps that consists of six centres with two transit camps at Muna and Customs House, both in Maiduguri. It is important to note that there are 379,614 IDP'S at 15 satellite camps comprising Ngala, Monguno, Bama, Banki, Pulka, Gwoza, Sabon Gari and other locations in the state. Unfortunately, 73,404 persons were forced to become refugees in neighbouring countries with Niger having 11,402 and Cameroon having 62,002 respectively.

A lecture delivered by a former governor stated:

> "We have an official record of 52,311 orphans who are separated and unaccompanied. We have 54,911 widows who have lost their husbands to the insurgency and about 9,012 have returned back to various communities of Ngala, Monguno, Damboa, Gwoza and Dikwa."

The good leadership of the Governor of Borno State, Professor Babagana Zullum brought so many changes to the challenges of the people. The governor visited Chad and sought the repatriation of 120,000 Nigerians refugees there back home. He also rebuilt many villages that were destroyed by the insurgents.

The Operation LAFIYA DOLE in the North East has been very successful. Troops conducted several clearance operations, aggressive patrols and Intelligence Surveillance Reconnaissance missions. Air offensive operations against Boko Haram/Islamic State in West Africa Province (ISWAP) terrorists led to the destruction of their camp and neutralisation of their commanders/leaders and other fighters. The Air Task Force launched coordinated air offensives on terrorists' camp at Ngwuri Gana Village, along Gulumba Gana-Kumshe axis in the Northern part of Borno State. The massive airstrikes led to the destruction of the terrorists' camp while several terrorists were neutralised. Additionally, the Land Component of Operation LAFIYA DOLE successfully conducted intelligence-based clearance operations that dealt devastating blows on the BHT/ISWAP terrorist elements in some parts of the North East. During these offensives, caches of arms and ammunition and other items were recovered, while several insurgents surrendered.

Significantly, troops of Operation SAHEL SANITY have recorded good strides flushing out bandits from Sokoto, Katsina and Zamfara States. The military's anti-Crude Oil Theft (COT) and other economic sabotage operation in the Niger Delta region. The Maritime Component of Operation DELTA SAFE recorded tremendous successes against economic saboteurs with the Nigerian Navy Ship PATHFINDER patrol team, using drones, discovered an illegal refining site around Cawthorne Channel and other places within the Niger Delta region. The desperation in the enormous oil theft in the region has forced the military to step up its operations in this places. This is very encouraging.

Establishment of Universities

One of the very outstanding performance of the Armed Forces in the Fourth Republic was the establishment of tertiary institutions that could be very useful for research purposes as it concerned the particular service. The Nigerian Army University is located in Mongono. This has helped to bring lots of development to the people within that region. The Admiralty University is located at Ibusa which is 20 km from Asaba, the Delta State Capital. The main objective is to expand the frontiers of knowledge in various field of studies that are unique specialization in maritime, logistics etc. It provides research that meet the social, scientific, economic and lots of other fields that have to do with maritime challenges. The Air Force Institute of Technology was upgraded. It is currently a Federal University in Nigeria with a mixture of both military and civilian students and workers. The projection is to have aircraft engineers and other technical specialists trained locally to save foreign exchange for the country.

The Nigerian Army under President Muhammadu Buhari

Introduction

The Nigerian Army is the oldest of the three services. Its inception was long before the country got her independence in 1st October 1960. The Nigerian Army has carried out tremendous exploits to maintain the unity of the country in line with the constitution of the Federal Republic of Nigeria. Although the Nigerian Army has had lots of criticisms from some political gladiators and educationists, the fact remains that the invaluable sacrifice of the Nigerian Army has kept the country in one piece as against the expectations of many detractors. Many international conspiracies have been nipped to the bud by the effort of the Nigerian Army.

There was so much demand for the service chiefs appointed by President Muhammadu Buhari to be changed a few years after the security challenges in the country began to deteriorate. The security problems were overwhelming. It is important to note that traditionally, the concept of security in the social sciences has been defined in reference to socio-political integration, namely a relationship between a community and a communal security provider. This is different in the Westphalian world which is dominated by Western political thought. In the case with our setting, the state owes the citizens the social contract law to protect them. In the Western world, this relationship has been conceptualised as being between citizen, state and statutory security provider. Going back to the idea of the Social Contract as a reciprocal security arrangement between society and state, security was to be provided by the state as a public good for society, as a fiduciary association. The very legitimacy of the state was tied to its ability to provide security as a public good inclusively to all members of the community, i.e. the nation.

When the government of President Muhammed Buhari came into power in 2015, the security situation of the country had already deteriorated. President Jonathan affirmed then that some members of the Boko Haram Sect had infiltrated his government. This made the challenge that started during the People Democratic Party's Government complex and difficult to understand. With an initial fire arms and military hardware purchase scandal legacy from the previous regime, the government of President Muhammadu Buhari began his regime by quickly purchasing military armaments for the Armed Forces of Nigeria. This was done to quickly change the tide of consistent security challenges. According to President Muhammadu Buhari:

> "Our tasks as the guardians of the nation are to prepare for the evolving and complex security situations and make sure that no terrorists can threaten Nigeria's sovereign integrity. When this Government came in 2015, we inherited a country at crossroads, with bombs going off with frightening frequency even in our cities, and we came in to confront and manage the crisis."

The Nigerian Army began to carry out attacks into the strongholds of Boko Haram destroying and neutralizing many of them and causing many of them to flee to the neighbouring countries like Chad, Cameroun, Niger Republic and Sudan. These are some of the remarkable achievements of the Nigerian Army under Lt Gen Tukur Burattai and Lt Gen Faruk Yahaya respectively.

Reclaiming Captured Local Governments

One of the deadly exploits of the Boko Haram Sect was their total destruction of villages and towns as well as taking full control of many of them. Some of the emirs and chief had to flee for their lives. The Sect imposed taxes on the people taking over the wives of many and turning the husband into forced fighters.

Unlike the years before President Buhari, a number of local governments were no-go-areas. Today, indigenes have safely returned back to Gwoza, Askira-Uba, Dikwa, Ngala, Monguno, Kukawa, Damboa, Konduga and Mafa. They are led by their traditional leaders. No one could ever visit these places or stay there. Emirs were all in exile. Today, captured towns have been reclaimed and have come back to life. So is Askira-Uba, Damboa, Gwoza and others. Life is has returned to Baga. What the Nigerian Army did was to deploy its troops close to these towns with very close surveillance making it difficult for the Boko Haram Sect to penetrate.

Reliable Synergy with other Services and Agencies

One of the viable characteristics of the Systems Theory is that all the parts must work together as a whole. Any disconnect from any of the parts will hamper the total functioning of the System. One of the schools of thought about the total outburst for the change in baton of the Armed Forces was the lack of synergy between the services especially the NA and NAF. There were lack of coordinated air support which rather than assist the ground troops caused own catastrophes.

Suffice to state here that, prior to the government of President Muhammadu Buhari, it was not possible to move a few kilometres out of Maiduguri. Insurgents were so bold to attack and take over military facilities, like the Army Barracks at Monguno, Bama, Giwa Barrack and Multinational Joint Task Force Headquarters at Baga, to mention just a few. There were daily bomb blasts in many parts of Maiduguri, the state capital and most populated part of the state.

Significantly, with President Muhammadu Buhari's government effort to equip the military, over two hundred kidnapped victims have been rescued by troops of Operation LAFIYA DOLE. A total of 1,385 rounds of ammunition, 45 grenades as well as 95 assorted rifles were recovered from BHT/ISWAP fighters. In addition, several gun trucks were captured, while some others were destroyed during air strikes. Furthermore, 1,805 insurgents/terrorists including commanders were killed by troops aside scores killed through air raids/attacks. Additionally, 79 arrests were made including high value targets. These criminals have been in the insurgency market within the Sahel region.

At the Operation DELTA SAFE, total of 8,890,300 litres of stolen diesel and 33,516,000 litres of kerosene were impounded by troops. Troops immobilised 185 illegal refining sites, 85 dugout pits and 163 metal storage tanks within the period. Additionally, troops impounded 31,236.8 barrels of stolen crude oil as well as 12,272,652 litres of stolen petrol from oil thieves in the Zone. Also, 47 kidnapped victims were rescued, while 72 vandals and criminals were arrested. A total of 4,250 bags of 50kg foreign parboiled smuggled rice were impounded and 45 boats engaged in illegal activities were impounded. Troops also arrested 53 pirates, impounded 25 trucks and recovered 23 rifles, 65,330 rounds of ammunition and destroyed 23 pirate camps. Troops of Operation AWATSE in the South-West Zone between 18 March and 30 December 2020, impounded 10,458,600 litres of petrol; 15,345 barrels of stolen crude oil and 345,000 litres of stolen diesel. Also, troops recovered 3,594 rounds of ammunition and 14 assorted rifles. Within the period, 23 illegal refining sites were immobilised, while 15 boats and 23 trucks engaged in illegal activities were impounded. In the same vein, 35 kidnap victims were rescued, while 48 arrests were made.

Under Operation HADIN KAI, a combination of kinetic and non-kinetic operations, coupled with a review of strategies, led to the neutralization of over 1000 terrorists, rescue of 2000 civilians and the surrender of over 22,000 terrorists including their families. Several arms and ammunition were also recovered. This is in addition to destruction of several IED/bomb making factories of the ISWAP/BHT. Under Operation HADARIN DAJI in the North West, the conduct of offensive clearance operations, raids and air operations resulted in the neutralization of about 427 bandits, arrest of 257 bandits, rescue of 897 civilians and recovery of 3,087 livestock. Similarly, Operation WHIRL PUNCH covering parts of Kaduna neutralized about 215 bandits, arrested 133 bandits, rescued 296 civilians and recovered 136 livestock, while Operation THUNDER STRIKE neutralized 36 bandits, arrested 74, rescued 296 civilians and recovered 136 livestock. In the North Central, raids and clearance operations conducted by Operation SAFE HAVEN neutralized 91 criminal elements, arrested 155 suspects, rescued 159 civilians and recovered 3,259 livestock. These efforts were achieved with the commitment of the Nigerian Army which has suffered more casualties than the other services.

Revitalisation of the Multi-National Joint Task Force

President Muhammadu Buhari saw the need for cooperation of countries with the Lake Chad Commission interest and other neighbours. The spate of terrorism activities and violence assumed such an alarming dimension that President Muhammadu Buhari decided to travel to N'Djamena the capital of Chad to discuss with the President of Chad Mahamat Derby whose father, President Idriss Derby was killed in a military operation by rebels in Chad. In the context of a globalised world, the state-centric approach to security appears to be old-fashioned – not least in the developing world. Socio-political integration no longer exclusively revolves around society and state. Instead, it is a transnational integration of communities and identities, with states as traditional public security providers finding it difficult to live up to their social contractarian duties. This had been defined in reference to concepts of national territoriality. For this study, it is very important.

It was agreed that the Multinational Joint Task Force (MNJT) be revamped. The task force now has troops from Benin Republic, Cameroon, Chad, Niger and Nigeria. Its mandate is to bring the Boko Haram insurgency to an end. The MNJTF which was once commanded by the former Chief of Defence Staff (CDS), Gen LEO Irabor in 2018 got better with his understanding of the challenges and further support on the mandate for the complete expulsion of Boko Haram anywhere in the world. These current exploits became possible with the passion of Maj Gen Abdul Khalifa Ibrahim which this study recommends to be an amiable quality leadership and Patriotic Citizenship example for the Nigerian State. The MNJTF in his tenure, continued to sustain its operations across the Lake Chad Basin to ensure the terrorists threats is brought to an end. These successful operations were able to reinforce the successes of the operations in Maiduguri. The capital of the MNJTF is N'Djamena. The MNJTF is unique and driven with a mandate to passion end Boko Haram. The commander of the joint task force is usually from the Nigerian Army. Suffice to state here that although Benin Republic participated in the operation with a company of troops earlier, only a few staff officers now work in the MNJTF Headquarters'. They do not have a sector. Besides, they are not a member of the Lake Chad Basin Commission. The MNJTF had a change in command in April, 2023. The new commander who is a crack military Patriotic Citizenship in the person of Maj Gen Gold Chubuisi kept the flag flying until a recent redeployment that now has Maj Gen IS Ali as the new commander. Maj Gen IS Ali's who was the former Theater Commander in Maiduguri has had many military exploits. Both Gen Gold Chubuisi and Gen IS Ali will certainly enhance the success story of the fight against Boko Haram. The two previous and new COAS have certainly done well to which this study holds in high esteem.

Sector 1 Cameroun: A significant operation was carried out here after a major intelligence driven Amphibious manoeuvre. This was conducted from 12 -16 September 2022. It was also a timely operation to 22 suspected Boko Haram locations in TCHOLLS, MORDAS, NAIRA, KASSOUAN MARIA, LOKO LIBI, NEMERY, KATIKINE, DORO LIMAN, BOUARAM, MANGALME, BLARAM, KOFIA and LOKO ISLANDS 1 and 2. Many of the Boko Haram logistics items and camps were destroyed during the operation. This made it difficult for many of them to regroup.

Sector 2 Chad: Chadian forces carried out Amphibious clearance operation on 13 August, 2022 to Hiba located South of Dabantchali following a detailed intelligence on the presence of Boko Haram in the Area. Unfortunately, the terrorists fled the area before the assault. Part of the challenge for troops is that the local are also part of the Boko Haram informants.

Sector 3 Nigeria: In this sector, several successful operations were carried out after good intelligence. A total number of 21 major logistics couriers and spies were arrested along the Damasak – Gubio – Monguno – Baga Axes from the Lake Chad Islands. Also, on 9 September 2022, Nigerian troops recovered 53 cows and arrested one Boko Haram during a raid at Musaram. On 11 September 2022, 5 Boko Haram Terrorists (BHT) vendors were intercepted in Monguno while trying to move fishing materials and food items into Lake Chad.

Additionally, it was reported that on 12 September 2022, two Boko Haram spies were arrested in Monguno. In the same stance, on 17 September 2022, the Nigerian troops at Kekeno arrested 3 Boko Haram Logistics couriers illegally transporting 4500 litres of Petrol towards Doron Baga. Similarly, on 23 September 2022 troops deployed at a check point in Monguno intercepted 2 suspected Boko Haram spies with their uniforms concealed inside a vehicle. On 26 September 2022, a Boko Haram informant and Fish vendor known as Abdulahi Saleh was arrested while trying to leave Monguno. The sum of Three

Hundred and Ten Thousand Naira (N310,000) was recovered from him. Likewise, on 28 September 2022 troops arrested 5 suspected Boko Haram spies when a raid was conducted in Monguno. On the same day 3 Boko Haram logistics Couriers were intercepted along Damasak – Gubio road while moving a huge consignment of dried Fish from the Lake Chad Island for sale in Maiduguri.

Sector 4 Niger: There were also successful operations in this sector which had very reliable and detailed Intelligence between August and September. A total of 40 Boko Haram logistics couriers were arrested along the Maine Soroa – Diffa – Garin Dogo – Kabalewa Axis. Also, on 16 August 2022 troops deployed at Kabalewa effected the arrest of one Moussa Abdoulaye at the Fish Market while trying to move some jerricans of Petrol into the Lake Chad. He was also in possession of Four Hundred and Twenty Thousand Naira(N420,000). The operation led to the arrest of another accomplice, Mudasir Ismail in Kano Nigeria on 22 August 2022.

In the same vein, on 24 and 25 August 2022, troops deployed along Garin Dogo – Kabalewa Axis intercepted 5 vehicles conveying food stuff and boat making materials into the Lake Chad. This led to the arrest of 32 suspects in connection with the movement. Then, on 7 September 2022 troops deployed at Geskerou intercepted 3 Boko Haram fighters trying to move to the Lake Chad from Sambisa Forest. All these operations made it very difficult for Boko Haram to move in mass. On 7 September 2022, troops of the sector successfully rescued abducted victims at Kenembouri and Kindjandi. The samething took place on 9 September, 2022 at N'Garoua Gana. Also, on 16 September 2022 troops from Bula Brin rescued some abducted victims and recovered vehicles and logistics which were carted away from commuters along Road Nguigmi – Bula Brin. These operations helped to totally dominate the ground forcing many of the terrorists to flee while some of them who are Nigerians decided to surrender. They could not find safety in any of the neighbouring countries.

Success Acknowledgement to Locals

The successes of the MNJTF is hinged on the vital and timely information from the members of the local population and the public in general. This has facilitated the flow of information for prompt action by troops. The successes achieved so far is helping to prevent the terrorist from carrying out any major attack on military and civilian targets within the Lake Chad Basin. This has brought relative peace and security within the area. The MNJTF also request that the activities of the terrorists within and around the communities must be reported. They must urgently report anyone trying to supply canoe, engine parts, food, cloth or fuel to the terrorists or any collaboration with the latter.

Relocation of the Military Command and Control Centre to Maiduguri in June 2015

Immediately after President Muhammadu Buhari ascended the throne, he moved the Military Command and Control Centre(MCCC) from Abuja to Maiduguri. According to the President, war cannot be fought from the nation's capital. This made it very easy for the service chiefs and key actors in the fight against insurgency to play their parts appropriately with constant on the ground synergy which has helped a lot in the battle.

Public secondary schools resumed in Borno on Monday 26 Sept 2016, after two years of closure

It is important to state here that the Boko Haram activities in the North East especially Bornu State made it necessary for schools to be closed. The spate of violence by these ruthless sect was such that the government had to direct the closure of all schools within the state until there was respite. Today, all the schools have resumed with adequate security in place to protect them.

Establishment of more Formations and Units

The Nigerian Army has expanded in strength and formations due to the security situation that seems to be everywhere in the country. The country currently has more divisions with brigades and battalions of different military classifications. This has increased the military dominance of the Nigeria State. It is so with the Nigerian Navy and Nigerian Air Force with Naval unit in Baga, a new Air base in Maiduguri and Katsina and many others. The current Nigerian Army Divisions are as underlisted:

1 Mechanized Division — HQ in Kaduna

2 Mechanized Division — HQ in Ibadan

3 Armoured Division — HQ in Jos

6 Amphibious Division — HQ in Port Harcourt

7 Infantry Division (OP-LD) — HQ in Maiduguri

8 Task Force Division — HQ in Sokoto

New Weapons, Military Hardwares and Personnel

The Nigerian Army under President Muhammadu Buhari has been tremendously equipped. This has raise the level of its operational readiness and efficiency, in addition to boosting its capacities. The Nigerian Army has received more than 2000 units of various Armoured Fighting Vehicles, guns, and equipment. During the period under review, the Nigerian Army procured 160 MRAPS, 150 trucks and 60 APCs to improve its equipment holding. Various kits were equally provided for troops. This is in addition to the provision of accommodation for troops and the recruitment of over 10,000 personnel into the Army.

Civil Appreciation and Award to two Nigerian Army Generals

Awards were conferred on the two Army Generals, Major Gen Maj Gen Abdul-Khalifah Ibrahim and Maj Gen Christopher Gwabin Musa by a media platform known as the Spye Communications Limited (SpyeTV), a Counter Insurgency media communication company in Nigeria. The Managing Director of the firm, Olayemi Esan stated that the awards were in recognition of the twosome's track record of selfless service, professionalism, distinguished and exceptional meritorious service to the nation while serving in positions of great responsibilities as war commanders. She reiterated that, the senior officers exhibited outstanding performance as commanders of the national and multinational joint task forces in the ongoing counter-insurgency operations in the North East and Lake Chad region.

She added that their leadership and personal sacrifices have significant impact in the success so far recorded in the ongoing operations as their actions and media relations are in keeping with the finest traditions of military service. The Managing Director further reiterated that when MNJTF re-operationalised with an increased capacity of about 10,000 troops, the force commander has since created a safe and secure environment in the areas affected by the activities of Boko Haram and other terrorist groups. She added that the successes recorded so far were due to cooperation at all levels driven by the leadership skills of both Generals to collectively fight insecurity in the region. This enabled the implementation of overall stabilisation programmes within the limit of its capabilities, humanitarian operations, and the delivery of assistance to the vulnerable population.

National Awards for the Military by the Nigerian State

With the laudable achievements of the Chief of Defence Staff, Gen LEO Irabor and his team of Service Chiefs as well as outstanding senior officers, the country had no other way of reward other than to include them in the national honours for Nigerians who have distinguished themselves in various works of life. This very important for this book as it portrayed Patriotic Citizenship and Service to the Nigerian State. The most outstanding in the award for the military was that of Maj Gen SA Adebayo who was the Chief of Defence Intelligence. Maj Gen CG Musa, the new Chief of Defence Staff and Maj Gen AK Ibrahim were also awarded. Previous awards were made last year in honour of all the Service Chiefs, Maj Gen JGK Myam, the Chief of Army Staff who died in a plane crash along with Brig Gen AU Kuliya, Brig Gen OL Olayinka and a few others. This, for this study is Patriotic Citizenship. Giving awards to individuals with no relevant impact the the Nigerian State is of no significance for this study.

Repentant and reintegration of Misled Nigerians in Boko Haram

Like what we had in the Niger Delta where our young adults got engaged into numerous arms fighting crimes, this study abhors the compulsory conscription of children and young adults into Boko Haram. Most of them were forced into hard drug such as cocaine etc. Certainly, they were brain washed with wrong doctrines making it difficult for them to believe in Patriotic Citizenship which this study stands for. Maj Gen CG Musa, who served as the 11th Theatre Commander Operation Hadi Kai in the North East, enhanced the amnesty programme for repentant terrorists. He made sure that the core values of the military were upheld with passionately driven efforts. Under Maj Gen CG Musa's command, over 47,975 terrorists and their families surrendered to troops. This made it necessary to have a programme.

The de-radicalisation, rehabilitation and reintegration programme for the regular the repentant Boko Haram was well packaged one. They were called clients. They were trained in batches. On arrival at the Disarmament, Demobilization and Reintegration (DRR) camp for the mandatory de-radicalisation, rehabilitation and reintegration programme, their data were captured by the National Identity Management Commission. They were then subjected to comprehensive physical and medical test by a combined team of medical experts from the Disarmament, Demobilization and Reintegration camp clinic and Federal Teaching Hospital Gombe. The medical tests were aimed at ascertaining the health status of the clients towards providing proper and adequate care during the Disarmament, Demobilization and Reintegration training cycle. The clients were trained in skills for self-reliance after re-interpretation with their communities. Some trained as barbers while some trained in shoe making. Some clients went for welding as vocation of choice and some clients selected tailoring. A few others were trained in carpentry and laundry services. Point of note, all the clients participated in the mandatory integrated farming, training activities which includes agro, poultry and fish farming. The essence was to make them self-reliant in whatever they chose to do. Or have a combination of projects they intend to embark on.

Capture of Boko Haram Operational and Spiritual Headquarters'

A very important feat of the Nigerian Army was the capture of the Boko Haram Terrorist Headquarters' which was their strong point known as Camp Zero in the dreaded Sambisa forest in December 2016. This was a place where the terrorists had all sorts of weapons and ammunitions, gun trucks, anti-aircraft missile launchers etc. There was the need for the Nigerian Army to deny the terrorist the use of the forest by completely holding the ground after the capture and avoid the regrouping of the sect. Subsequently, the Nigerian Army conducted its Small Arms Championship in the forest from 26 – 31 March 2017 in the forest. Since then, several military activities have been conducted in the forest.

Safety Return of Activities

With the Nigerian Army dominating and holding the grounds in synergy with the Nigerian Navy and Air Force most parts of the North East have relative peace. It is for this reason that the Chairman of the Christian Association of Nigeria, Borno State Chapter declared the 2017 Easter Celebrations as the best and safest since 2009. This was very significant for people and investors coming into Maiduguri and other parts of the North East to do business.

Another important thing to note is that Arik Air resumed flights to Maiduguri in May 2017, three years after suspending operations to the city. Other flights followed with no fear of attacks.

Subsequently, with relative safety, the Nigerian Army reopened Maiduguri-Bama-Banki Road in March 2018, four years after it was seized by the Boko Haram terrorists.

Additionally, farmers and fishermen have returned to their professions with renewed hope for a better life. This is possible as thousands have returned back to their communities.

Good Christians and Moslems make Good Citizenship

Most Nigerians confess and believe in God Almighty by relentlessly standing against doctrines that are detrimental to the state. This study tries to re-echo what the Prophet TB Joshua of blessed memory said about true citizenship. The Prophet without mincing words adviced that we cannot claim that we honour the Lord God Almighty without being good citizens irrespective of the religion that we belong to. This makes it important for religious bodies to help to hold God's values and apply them to the oneness of the state. It is rather hypocritical to see Patriotic Citizenship taken for granted and in some cases turned to hate speeches and political dislike.

Trooping and Colour Presentation Parade

The Nigerian Army conducted the Trooping and Colour Presentation Parade at the Eagle Square, Abuja on the 27 April 2023. The retired national and regimental colours were marched off the drill square, marking the end of befitting service to their respective units and the nation, and the beginning of new colours. The President and Commander in Chief of the Armed Forces who was in uniform reviewed the parade. The retired national and regimental colours were taken to the Nigerian Army Museum Abuja for safekeeping and display. It is highest parade that the President reviewed before he left office.

The Nigerian Navy

The Achievements of the Nigerian Navy under President Muhammadu Buhari

Introduction

Nothing makes a fighting force outstanding other than the obvious fighting capabilities and fire power. There are numerous achievements of the Nigeria Navy since 2015. This places the President Muhammadu Buhari's regime score board on the Nigerian Navy very high. This study is of the view that the giant strides of the service like that of the Nigerian Army and the Nigerian Air Force is simply excellent. This is seen in the execution of its constitutional roles when compared with previous governments in the Fourth Republic. The two former Chiefs of Naval Staff, Vice Admiral Ibas and Vice Amiral Awwal Zubairu Gambo have thus satisfied what this study seek to promote in Patriotic Citizenship. These achievements will be discussed below.

66th Nigerian Navy Anniversary Celebration

One of the remarkable achievements of the Nigerian Navy was its the 66th Anniversary of the service which had many events that helped to boast Patriotic Citizenship. Nigerians could see the incredible contribution to the peace, progress, prosperity and global image of Nigeria as a nation. It is therefore, important that the legacy of service to the Nigerian State by the Navy justified this celebration. There was an International Maritime Conference and Regional Maritime Exercise (IMCREMEX) 2022. The Conference held at the Onne Port Multi-Purpose Centre, Rivers State with the theme, "Optimising Collaboration for Maritime Security and Socio-Economic Development in Africa." The Exercise was flagged off at the Federal Ocean Terminal, also in Onne, Rivers State. One of the key points of IMCREMEX 2022 was that it enhanced regional cooperation and boost effort towards collective security of the maritime domain. This is very important for synergy with other agencies that this study is particular about. The Special Guest of Honour at the Conference was His Excellency, President Muhammadu Buhari.

Operational Achievement

The Nigerian Navy has conducted over 40 operations from 2015 – till date. These have substantially improved security in Nigeria's waters during the period under review. These operations led to the arrest of over 492 vessels suspected of committing various infractions within the maritime domain. Recently, the Nigerian Navy participated in training exercises with at least 8 countries National Navies. These are; French, Brazilian, Royal Navy, Pakistani, Italian, Spanish, US and Canadian Navies. This is very important in the way the country is viewed by other nations in the world.

Collaborations with other countries

The Nigerian Navy collaborates with all navies in the Region under the auspices of the 2013 Yaoundé Code of Conduct, which prioritizes cooperation and information sharing between navies of Economic Community of West African States and Economic Community of Central African States. This is very important as it strengthen the safety of the maritime domain from seafarer criminals.

One very important aspect of international relations of this study is that of strategic collaboration. The Nigerian Navy has continually collaborated with International and Regional partners. The Service has collaborated with the International Police especially in the area of information gathering for actionable intelligence towards combating piracy and other crimes within Nigeria's maritime domain which led to the arrest of MV CHAYANEE NAREE in October 2021 for conveying 33kg of cocaine worth 1.5 million US Dollars from Brazil to Lagos.

Also, under the European Union-Coordinated Maritime Presence in the (Gulf of Guinea) GoG, the Navy collaborates with ships from European Union Navies to patrol the GoG towards addressing security challenges. Noteworthy is the first ever Joint Event on Strengthening Nigeria – EU Cooperation on Maritime Security which held in Lagos on 7 April 2022 with a view to solidifying the close partnership that has developed between the Nigerian Navy, the European Union and EU Member States operating in the region. Allied to these efforts are the annual multi-national maritime exercises such as Ex OBAN GAME EXPRESS and Ex GRAND AFRICAN NEMO sponsored by the United States of America and France respectively.

Moreover, under a new framework for tackling insecurity in the Gulf of Guinea (GoG) named the Gulf of Guinea Maritime Collaboration Forum and Shared Awareness De-confliction (GOG-MCF/SHADE), the Nigerian Navy with its high profile plays an active significant role. It is the lead agency responsible for maritime security in Nigeria. This collaboration is very important as it helps to tighten maritime security.

Reduced Piracy Incidents

The Nigerian Navy has done so well by reducing the incidents of piracy. Three dedicated NN operations, TSARE TEKU, CALM WATERS, RIVER SWEEP amongst others have reduced piracy incidences in Nigerian waters from 70 in 2016 to only one attack as at August 2022. This noble achievement was complemented by the International Maritime Bureau Global Piracy Report of 14 July 2021, which indicated the lowest number of piracy and sea robbery against ships in Nigeria waters in 27 years.

The report was corroborated by the Defence Web, which noted further decline in reported cases of piracy and armed attacks against shipping in Nigerian waters. That with the latest International Maritime Bureau report of 3 March 2022 shows that Nigeria has exited the IMB's Piracy List which means that Nigeria is no longer in the list of piracy prone countries which has many consequences and positive news for the shipping industry, general maritime commerce, and the national economy. This is very commendable which this study considers as Patriotic Citizenship strides.

Reduction in oil Theft Incidents and other Maritime Crimes

The Nigerian Navy anti-crude oil theft operations led to the arrest of a total of 4,486 suspected persons involved in crude oil theft. The Nigerian Navy has also performed satisfactorily in the fight against crude oil theft and illegal oil bunkering through operations conducted by operations bases and Forward Operating Bases (FOBs). The most recent and ongoing operation in the Nigerian Navy is Op DAKATAR DA BARAWO (meaning "Stop the Thief" in Hausa Language) which was activated on 1 April 2022. This operation was in synergy with the Nigerian National Petroleum Corporation Limited. It is important to state here that within 7 weeks, the operation recorded some successes. These operations led to the arrest of 45 suspects, deactivation of 172 Illegal Refining Sites (IRS), 745 metal storage tanks, 567 ovens, 263 pits including the destruction of 50 wooden boats and 14 speed boats. These are dangerous operations against die hard criminals who are very conversant with all water bodies, could sometimes experience shoot out.

The Nigerian Navy Patrol Teams were able to deprive the oil thieves of about 11,781,937 Liters of illegally refined AGO, 20,378,414 Liters (128,180 bbls) of crude oil and 367,715 Liters of DPK. Others are, about 232,000 Liters of PMS, 830,000 Liters of Sludge and 66,000 Liters of LPFO. These products are worth over Fifteen Billion, Seven Hundred and Sixty-One Million, Five Hundred and Thirty-Six Thousand Four Hundred and Forty Naira (N15,761,536,440). This is very commendable and should be sustained in the future. This study is of the view that all those involved in these criminal acts must be arrested and brought to justice.

In furtherance to the above feat, the Nigerian Navy also increased routine patrols within the last 7 years. This is from 2015 to August 2022. Subsequently, the Nigerian Navy ships have clocked annual average of 25,574 hours at sea. This has led to appreciable decrease in maritime related criminal activities within the maritime domain.

The Nigerian Navy has made considerable gains in its anti-smuggling operations within the period under review. These efforts redoubled in the past 7 years due to closer collaboration with other stakeholders under the auspices of Operation SWIFT RESPONSE. In support of national effort against the illegal importation of foreign rice, a total of 82,907 bags of foreign rice valued at about N2 Billion have been arrested so far. The Maritime Domain Awareness facilities made up of the Falcon Eye (established by the Federal Government Nigeria - Office of the National Security Adviser) and Regional Maritime Awareness Capability have greatly improved the Nigerian Navy's surveillance capacity while assisting in other roles to secure the country in other areas. Currently, it is important to note that the service carries out round the clock surveillance of Nigeria's maritime space using surface vessels, helicopters and the robust Maritime Domain Awareness infrastructure. This has increasingly assisted the Nigerian Navy's patrol efforts particularly quick response capability and effective tracking and arrest of many vessels involved in maritime related crimes. Details of Nigerian Navy's operational achievements from 2015 – 2022 will be shown at the end of this study.

Fleet Renewal and Procurements

Under President Muhammadu Buhari Administration, the Nigerian Navy witnessed extensive procurement of platforms of different types and mix. Some of the Progresses made by the Navy was in the areas of Fleet Recapitalization and operational activities. This was a top priority and was as a result of the unflinching support of the President Muhammadu Buhari through aggressive fleet recapitalization that led to acquisition of several capital ships which includes Fast Patrol Boats, Inshore Patrol Crafts including air assets as well as the indigenous construction of Seaward Defence Boats. The government funded the procurement of 381 flat bottomed, assault, rigid hull, riverine patrol and whaler boats. Importantly, about 200 of these riverine patrol boats were built in-country, thus complementing indigenous ship building capacity, employment generation and skills acquisition. These have greatly enhanced the Nigerian Navy.

With the successful commissioning of the second and third locally built Seaward Defence Boat (SDB) NNS KARADUWA in 2016 and NNS OJI in 2021, local-shipbuilding is being further enhanced through the indigenous construction of SDB IV and SDB V. These are the aspects of service in Patriotic Citizenship which this study stands for. It is helping to leave a legacy that stands for the future of the Nigerian Navy and the Nigerian State.

The Nigerian Navy has also deployed 14 Naval Security Stations along the nation's coastline in areas prone to illegalities under the Choke Point Regime and Control operations. Additionally, President Buhari administration facilitated the procurement of 16 fast attack craft, seaward defence boats and inshore patrol craft. Furthermore, 1 survey ship, 1 offshore patrol vessel and 1 landing ship tank have joined the Nigerian Navy fleet while 1 AW 139 LeonPardo helicopter has been delivered to the Service. Cumulatively, the fleet renewal effort of the Nigerian Navy within the period under review has led to the procurement of well over 415 platforms of various types and combination.

Furthermore, on 1 April 2022, the Nigerian Navy took delivery of its newly constructed Landing Ship Tank (LST)-100, NNS KADA at DAMEN Shipyard in Sharjah at the United Arab Emirates. Significantly, the Nigerian Navy recently signed a contract with DEARSAN Shipyard of Turkey for the construction of 2 X 76m High Endurance Offshore Patrol Vessels and also in the process of taking delivery of Unmanned Aerial Vehicles to enhance Nigeria Maritime Surveillance/Domain Awareness assets including Nigerian Navy response capability. It is important to state that the construction of SDB IV and V at Naval Dockyard Limited, Lagos has begun.

Hydrographic Survey Charting Ship Significance

Another excellent feat is the Nigerian Navy survey ship NNS LANA which has begun a systematically organized hydrographic survey and charting of the nation's coastal and offshore waters. The ship joined the fleet from France in December 2021, while the contract for another 35m Hydrographic Survey Ship has been signed with OCEA Shipbuilding, France. The landing ship tank, NNS KADA, recently returned back to Nigeria after its deployment to Guinea Bissau on ECOWAS mission. This is the first of its kind in the country to which this study sees as heartwarming and Patriotic Citizenship.

The Strategic Directive 5-2021 and the Nigerian Navy Strategic Plan 2021-2030.

To meet up with the contemporary strategic security environment, the Chief of Naval Staff promulgated the above strategic directives. These very important policy documents have refocused and re-energized the Nigerian Navy towards higher productivity and service delivery underpinned by the Nigerian Navy's core values of Integrity, Professionalism and Teamwork. These will assist future Chiefs of the Naval Staffs to have an easy sail while in office. This is Patriotic Citizenship which this study proffers.

The International Maritime Conference 2022

This very important conference featured the convergence of African Naval Chiefs and Maritime Security experts to discuss deeply and cross-examine as well as agree on modalities for fulfilling the requirements of the African Union Peace and Security Council (AU PSC) Communique 1012, in support of the 2050 African Integrated Maritime Strategy.

It is important to state here that the Communique did establish Combined Maritime Task Forces among the navies of the Gulf of Guinea (GoG) states and those along the Eastern/Southern coastlines as well as a Continental Maritime Advisory Council to be composed of the Heads of Navies and Coast Guards. It is such that the delegates to this year's conference were not limited to GoG states only but also those of Eastern and Southern African nations. This was a very good milestone to collaboration and strong ties among nations. Subsequently and very important too, several friendly nations had their ships to participate in the Regional Exercise Alongside Nigerian Navy ships and aircrafts.

Infrastructural Development

It is very important to state here that Nigerian Navy has done excellently on its capacity to effectively deliver on her mandate to protect the nation's maritime environment and motivate her personnel for improved output. Thus, the Service embarked on numerous infrastructural and welfare projects. These projects have helped to improve the lives of the personnel and their families. It is important to state here that over 300 constructions and related projects have been undertaken from 2015 - August 2022 with over 90 per cent of these projects completed and others are at various stages of completion. One of the significant infrastructural project is the reconstruction of NNS BEECROFT Jetty Apapa, Lagos. This project provides berthing facility for the bulk of Nigerian Navy ships within the Western Naval Command area of responsibility. It has made it easy for the Nigerian Navy to stay aloof other civil facilities.

Additionally, there are Jetties at Naval Shipyard Limited Port Harcourt, Under Water Warfare School Ojo, NOP KOLUAMA and other new Bases are at various stages of completion. These feats for this study is very important. The Nigerian Navy also completed the construction of an Utra-Modern Navy Sport Complex in Navy Town, Ojo, Lagos.

There are other remarkable achievements. The Nigerian Navy has also within the period under review engaged in the extensive housing development for personnel accommodations as well as other welfare projects. These include the construction of over 2,500 housing units across the country. Many of them have been completed and commissioned. Some of the completed projects include hundreds of Compressed Earth Bricks buildings at Atimbo Barracks in Calabar, Kuje Barracks in Abuja and NNS LUGARD in Lokoja. There are also various units of accommodation for officers and ratings at Kubwa, Navy Town Asokoro Abuja and Navy Town Lagos. Significantly, there are also projects close to completion in the Nigerian Navy. These are the construction of Nigerian Navy Logistics School at Dawakin Tofa Kano, Nigerian Navy Hotel and Suites Calabar, Naval War College permanent site and projection for the construction of facilities at the newly established Naval Bases at Ekpe, Lekki and Shagunu. The details of some Nigerian Navy projects and procurements from 2015 – 2022 is also shown in this study.

Human Resource Management and Administration

On this aspect of the study, it is important to state here that the Nigerian Navy has contributed immensely to human resource development in Nigeria through the establishment of Admiralty University of Nigeria (ADUN) Ibusa, Delta State, the Naval War College in Calabar and the Nigerian Navy Military School Ikot Ituen, in Akwa Ibom State respectively. Additionally, Nigerian Navy Primary and Secondary Schools have also been established in Kaduna, Bauchi, Rivers, Sokoto and Bayelsa States. The Nigerian Navy also commissioned the Naval Base in Lokoja and a 150 units' barracks in Banda, Lokoja, Kogi State. These have made it easy for its personnel to live within the bases rather than have a few of them live outside the base due to shortage of accommodations.

In 2018, President Muhammadu Buhari commissioned an ultramodern Nigerian Navy Reference Hospital in Calabar, after 40 years of neglect. The hospital was conceived to be the best in Africa at that time with some unique features. These among others includes the installation of Endoscope Suite at the Hospital to attend to critical surgical needs using 21st century equipment that ensure minimal access/invasive procedure. The Nigerian Navy has also constructed an Imaging Centre at Nigerian Navy Reference Hospital Ojo, Lagos and upgraded Nigerian Navy hospitals in Warri and Port Harcourt respectively with modern diagnostic equipment. Additionally, incompliance with the world's challenge and a timely intervention, the Nigerian Navy established a COVID-19 Treatment and Isolation Centre on 1st June 2020 in Lagos. This was to cater for Nigerian Navy personnel infected with the virus, in support of the national effort. It is important to state here that the efforts and results of the treatment only showed that the Nigerian Navy has come of age in medical expertise.

Innovative Training in Asymmetric Operations

Another aspect of great importance is that the Nigerian Navy has introduced some innovative training for its personnel. This also extends to sister services and other security agencies to enhance efficiency in asymmetric operations. Some of the trainings include Basic, Advanced and Tactical Riverine Operations trainings for Nigerian Navy Special Boat Service and Nigeria Navy Special Forces at the Joint Maritime Security Training Centre (JMSTC). The training is geared towards improving their capabilities for efficiency in operations environment. The Nigerian Navy conducted Pre-Deployment Training (PDT) at JMSTC for regular Nigerian Navy ratings involving boat handling and Basic Field Craft prior to deployment for the various internal Counter Terrorist and Counter Insurgency (CT/COIN) Operations namely; Ops HADARIN DAJI, WHIRL STROKE, HADIN KAI and WHIRL PUNCH. These have greatly improved the combat readiness of the service.

Furthermore, the Nigerian Navy established Joint Combined Exercises and Training (JCET) between the Nigerian Navy Special Boat Service and the United States Marine Corps. Significantly, the operations are basically Counter Terrorist and Counter Insurgency (CT/COIN) based, and subsequently replicated at the Nigerian Navy Special Boat Service Camp for other Nigerian Navy Special Boat Service operatives. Others are the Intermediate Operating Capability (IOC) training, which is also Counter Terrorist and Counter Insurgency (CT/COIN) based, for the Nigerian Navy Special Boat Service (NNSBS) by the UK Royal Marine Commandos at Joint Maritime Security Training Centre (JMSTC).

There were also Tactical Riverine Operating Capability (TROC) Courses/Trainings for Instructors of Nigerian Army Amphibious Training School, Defence Headquarters' SOF, Nigerians Air Force Regiment, Marine Police of Nigerian Police Force and Multi-Agency groups (Nigerian Army, Nigerian Navy, Police, Marine Customs, Marine NSCDC and NDLEA elements) at JMSTC between 2015 and 2022 respectively.

Suffice to state here that 50 trainees are undergoing Advanced Navy Special Forces at European Security Academy, Poland. As a way of encouraging Nigerian Navy ratings for their commitment, for the first time in history, the Nigerian Navy recently granted presidential concessional promotion to 12 senior rates to the rank of Lieutenants.

Other Milestone Giant Strides

This study commends the Nigerian Navy for these Patriotic Citizenship notable milestones. These were through capacity building in indigenous navigational chart production with the production of 2 indigenous navigational charts covering parts of Nigerian waters as well as operational charts covering the entire Niger Delta region. The Service has also commenced work on the production of electronic versions of these charts to facilitate their formal validation internationally and eventual release. This proficiency has enhanced operational activities across the Nation's maritime environment, particularly within the backwaters. Importantly, such improved hydrographic capacity has immensely contributed to enhancing the maritime business environment. This is evidence in the about 30 per cent improvement in the Nation's maritime trade in the past years. There is also a significant increase in oil and gas production in the country.

In addition to various tangible achievements over the last 7 years, there have been numerous intangible attainments, particularly in the areas of concepts and organisation. The introduction of the Harmonised Standard Operating Procedures on Arrest, Detention and Prosecution of Maritime Criminals has been a real game changer in enhancing cooperation among maritime law enforcement agencies under the leadership of the Nigerian Navy. Maritime jurisdiction has been further boosted by the President's assent of the Suppression of Piracy and other Maritime Offences Act, 2019. This is the first legal instrument in the entire West African region. It has gone a long way to foster discipline in the sector.

NIGERIAN NAVY MARITIME OPERATIONS DATA 2015 – 29 AUG 22

Serial	Description	2015	2016	2017	2018	2019	2020	2021	29 AUG 22	Total	Remarks
(a)	(b)	(c)	(d)	(e)	(f)	(g)	(h)	(i)	(j)	(k)	(l)
	PIRACY IN THE GULF OF GUINEA										
1.	Pirate attacks – GoG	34	89	55	70	47	44	11	1	351	
	ATTACKS IN NIGERIAN WATERS										
2.	Pirate attack in Nigeria Waters	17	70	48	36	21	22	11	1	226	
3.	Sea Robbery	5	29	14	20	23	16	3		110	
	COT										
4.	Qty of Crude Oil Destroyed (bbls)	158,528	646,983	218,059	295,028	296,192	1,522,087	1,664,628.61	733,536.03	5,535,042	
5.	Qty of AGO Destroyed (MT)	1,403	348,450	53,587	29,969	28,326	539,829	45,752.91	32,767.80	1,080,085	
6.	Qty of PMS Destroyed (litres)	1,133,052	176,675	327,811	800,000	132,759	21,610	66,920	245,025.00	2,903,852	
7.	Qty of DPK Destroyed (litre)	6,700	39,760	374,000	162,500	2,702,000	289,400	4,638,751	14,431,170.00	22,644,281	
	DETAILS OF ARRESTED PERSONS INVOLVED IN COT AND SMUGGLING										
8.	Arrested Suspects	1,045	784	659	543	711	487	86	171	4,486	
	IRS										
9.	Illegal Refineries Destroyed	608	181	1,822	637	869	982	268	374	5,741	
	DETAILS OF ARRESTED VESSELS AND BARGES										
10.	Arrested Vessels	47	55	70	64	81	88	44	43	492	
(a)	(b)	(c)	(d)	(e)	(f)	(g)	(h)	(i)	(j)	(k)	(l)
11.	Arrested Barges	81	50	120	64	81	43	11	3	442	
12.	Arrested Speed Boats	11	135	151	104	73	57	10	34	575	

Conclusion

This study is impressed with the combat readiness of the Nigerian Navy which saw a supersonic boast during the government of President Muhammadu Buhari. It commends the two service chiefs for the remarkable exploits within the period under review. This is the Patriotic Citizenship and Service to which this study craves for. There is therefore, the need for the impending service chief to maintain this standard or improve on it. Although, this is certain as the new Chief of Naval Staff is an outstanding and excellent personality, Patriotic Citizenship should be strongly encouraged to make Nigeria great.

The Nigerian Air Force

The Nigerian Air Force Under President Muhammadu Buhari

Introduction

This study looked at the achievements of the two Chiefs of Air Staff especially the Chief of Air Staff within the second phase of President Muhammadu Buhari's government. Air Marshal Oladayo Amao became the 21st Chief of the Air Staff (CAS). It will be remembered that the country had many people especially the political elites urging the President of Nigeria to replace the service chiefs that had been with him for over six years. While some schools of thought opined that the drive to totally annihilate the insurgency lacked some new ideas, it became obvious that a change in baton was necessary. The Nigerian Air Force under the new leadership decided to leverage on credible partnership, while focusing on enhancing professionalism so as to promote performance and motivate initiatives that would create an enabling environment for successful operations. This became very important considering the increasing and menacing activities as well as the utterances and video clips sent to the social media by the criminal terrorist leaders.

The main strategic thrust of the Chief of Air Staff was hinged on synergising and partnering with the sister services and other security agencies as well as the generality of stakeholders, towards achieving the Nigerian Air Force goal of maintaining peace, law, and order. This is totally in line with the Systems Theory that is conceptualized here to meet the excellent performance of the new service chiefs. This is further reiterated with the fact that since the nature of war continues to evolve, regular doctrines embedded in the fundamentals and principles of war have basically remained the same but with some little addition as regards the wars on insurgents and guerilla warfare generally. Thus, the Nigerian Air Force decided to collaborate with her sister services, the Nigerian Army and Nigerian Navy as well as other security agencies in re-strategizing and use the best approaches of tackling current national security challenges which are extremely different from that of conventional warfare.

During the past approaches, it was observed that there was lack of synergy between the ground troops and the Nigerian Air Force which at that time focused predominantly on attaining air superiority without adequate commitment to ground troops. This led to many mishaps and did not translate to strategic advantages towards operational successes. Therefore, the Chief of Air Staff decided that in critically applying the principles of war, personnel motivation and inter-service cooperation should stand out as a time-tested doctrine capable of bringing the Armed Forces of Nigeria (AFN) closer to achieving the core mandate of securing the nation. This, he envisaged as the best way forward in achieving the mandate of the President and Commander in Chief of the Armed Forces. It must be stated here that with so many terrorists' groups and ethnic militias with separatist agendas, the Nigereian Air Force has a lot of tasks along with ground troops as these criminals' roam across the ungoverned landscape of the country killing and inflicting serious injuries on the vulnerable and poor citizens. While there is a strong determination to have the Nigerian Air Force functioning as an interdependent team of land, sea and air forces, requiring application of closely integrated efforts to accomplish assigned military objectives, a lot more jointness is required, to keep the tempo. Thus, the Chief of Air Staff was of the view that cross domain synergy was ultimately about evolving the understanding of jointness which enables more effective combination and utilisation of capabilities of the various services in joint operating environment. This has made room for the Patriotism Citizenship that this studies puts forward. Thus the vision of the Chief of Air Staff was for the Nigerian Air Force, 'To enhance and sustain critical airpower capabilities required for joint force employment in pursuit of national security imperatives.' This has tremendously helped to propel the drive while emphasis on doctrinal development and application of air power in joint military operations, purposeful training and human capacity development as well as platforms and equipment serviceability through innovative maintenance methods and logistics support systems are the main pivot for sustainable focus. While there is a clear and tremendous synergy between the services which the Chief of Air Staff ensured that he maintained, he warranted that there must be a disciplined workforce essential for combat readiness and bolstering troop morale by improving personnel welfare. No wonder, so much was achieved within a short time.

Remarkable Strides

The call for the change of service chiefs was like an outcry that needed to be taken seriously by the President and Commander in Chief of the Federal Republic of Nigeria even though with some reluctance. However, it was well appreciated with tremendous achievements within a short time. The Nigerian Air Force recorded very significant achievements in the fight against insurgency, terrorism, banditry, kidnapping and other forms of criminal activities in the country. It was difficult for these criminals to operate openly without cover as it was in the past. More sophisticated weapons and intelligence were used to bring them out of their hideouts. Additionally, the acquisition of new platforms, reactivation of existing ones as well as effective, synergistic and collaborative efforts with sister security agencies made the Nigerian Air Force the nation's pride.

The issues of terrorism have kept many countries on their toes. Nigeria experienced a steady increase in terrorist attacks in 2011, particularly in the northern states of Bornu, Yobe, Bauchi, Gombe, Plateau, Kaduna as well as the Federal Capital Territory. However, the second phase of the President Muhammadu Buhari's government witnessed a period of an improvement in cooperation and synergy among the services which has yielded so much remarkable outcomes that are acknowledged by many. For instance, there have been air strikes at Marte, the Tumbuns on the Lake Tchad and Malam Fatori in the Northeast where several the Islamic State in West Africa Province (ISWAP) terrorists and their followers were eliminated. This is a testimony to the renewed vigour and synergy that the Nigerian Air Force and the Nigerian Army have brought to bear which was lacking in the previous service chiefs' dispensation. This study is of the view that no service should work independently in the fight against insurgents or in the pursuit of the safety of the corporate existence of the Nigerian State. The understanding of the Systems Theory has provided the synergy that is required to achieve the desired mandate of the Armed Forces.

The coordinated operations by the Nigerian Air Force, Nigerian Army, Department of State Security and the Nigerian Police Force have led to the elimination of key terrorists and bandits in the North West including the notorious Alhaji Auta and Kachalla Ruga, among other terrorists and hardened criminals who have pestered the local people persistently for months. It is significant to add here that the achievements came as though it was not the same scenario on the ground after the downwards turn of events.

In furtherance to these strides, the Nigerian Air Force Special Forces elements have been reinvigorated and further given advanced training both at home and abroad to confront the current security challenges in the country as they fight side by side with other services Special Forces and security agencies in the various Theatres of Operation.

As though these supporting joint operations are too tasking, the Nigerian Air Force has also conducted independent operations to destroy insurgents' capabilities before they can be brought to bear on own forces. These proactive attacks have humbled these hardened criminal terrorist groups many of who are fighters that roam the troubled zones of Africa. These efforts forced the remnants of unrepentant terrorist elements to be neutralised to enable the Patriotic Citizenship hopefuls to carry out their legitimate aspirations without fear or intimidation as was obtainable in the past.

Developmental Doctrines

The former Chief of Air Staff has tried to ensure sustainable template, a common frame of reference on the most effective approach to air power employment. These are legacies that will be on for a long time with renewed efforts. The Nigerian Air Force has developed 11 new doctrines within such a short time. This is commitment to service and what truly Patriotic Citizenship stands for. Let me state here that all of these could not have been achieved without the leadership and vision of the then Chief of Defence Staff, Gen LEO Irabor who encouraged and ensured that Patriotic Citizenship is the watch word to the service of the Nigerian State. This was through effective leadership and a System Theory driven military under his supervision to accomplished a flawless National Security standard.

Suffice to state here that the development of the doctrines is in tandem with one of the key drivers of the then Chief of Air Staff vision which is, "Focus on doctrinal development and application of air power in joint military operations." Additionally, these doctrines are essentially based on analysis of the contemporary security environment as well as the operational experiences of the service which is very unique and deadly in the face of any form of threat. Thus, all relevant competencies in the Nigerian Air Force are now guided by updated doctrines especially the planning, allocation and sustainment of Nigerian Air Force air efforts. This is an invaluable contribution to service.

Fleet Acquisition

The President Muhammed Buhari's government increased the capacity of the Armed Forces much more than any government in the Fourth Republic. Under Air Marshal Amao, the Nigerian Air Force has witnessed a tremendous boost to its aircraft holdings across various fleets. This has significantly changed the military might of the Armed Forces. Apart from the previously acquired platforms which the Nigerian Air Force had, in 2021 alone, there were 15 brand new aircraft and Unmanned Combat Aerial Vehicles (UCAV) were taken delivery of to boost the fire power of the Nigerian Air Force. Also, the reactivation of hitherto unserviceable platforms to upscale its capabilities in tackling all forms of criminality have been successfully carried out.

It is very important to state here that the latest additions of 3 JF-17 Thunder multi-role fighter aircraft and 12 A-29 Super Tucano aircraft recently inducted into the Nigerian Air Force Order of Battle are presently deployed in various theatres of operation across the country to add impetus to the ongoing war against insurgency, armed banditry and other forms of criminality in the country. This has tremendously increased the fire power of the Nigerian Air Force.

There is also the acquisitions and reactivation as well as the emplacement of robust logistics support structures. These have enabled the Nigerian Air Force to raise the serviceability status of operable aircraft from about 35 per cent (35 per cent) in 2015 to about 72 per cent. This is as at 27 December 2021. Significantly, the deployment of these platforms for combat has brought some level of sanity and normalcy to previously terrorist/bandits ravaged areas in the North-East and North-West as many of these criminal met their death with ease. The Nigerian Air Force has lately started to function efficiently as a highly technical service and a fighting force for the effective defence of Nigeria's territorial integrity.

Trainings of Personnel

With all the list of achievements earlier stated, the Nigerian Air Force has boosted the capacity of its Regiment and Special Forces with additional training and equipment to improve operations in the fight against insurgency and other forms of criminality across the country. The service has also heightened its recruitment drive by graduating additional 1,031 recruits at the Military Training Centre in Kaduna. To further enhance its training, the Nigerian Air Force sent 10 Senior Non-Commissioned Officers of the ranks of Air Warrant Officer and Master Warrant Officer to the United Kingdom for a unique 4-part international pre-retirement training.

Aircraft engineering are aimed at enhancing operational effectiveness. To this end, the Aircraft Engineering Branch made concerted efforts to secure some foreign training slots for Nigerian Air Force engineers. This has enhanced the required efficiencies.

It is important to state here that some of the trainings undertaken by the branch include conduct of in-house aircraft battery maintenance and training at 107 Air Maritime Group, training of 7 aircraft engineers on PT-6A engine rigging for King Air 350 aircraft in the United States of America. Additionally, the training of 5 Nigerian Air Force aircraft engineers on DO-228 aircraft engine rigging in Germany and the conduct of 'Train the Trainer Course' for 13 engineers at Nigerian College of Aviation Technology, Zaria. All these have added up to give the Nigerian Air Force it current outstanding rating.

Fresh Wings

The Nigerian Air Force has produced winged 56 pilots and operators who graduated from various pilot courses both at home and abroad. Additionally, several officers, airmen and airwomen of the Nigerian Air Force have been sent to different types of training in various countries including the United States of America, South Africa,

India, Belgium, Egypt and Pakistan, amongst others. This has turned around what the Nigerian Air Force was in the past.

Let us delve into other significant strides. These include the conduct of Master Technician Course at Flight Safety International Wichita, USA, Advance Maintenance training on Mi-35P helicopter by Ukrainian Technical Team at 115 Special Operations Group, Port Harcourt, Conduct of Avionics Components Repair Course at Central Avionics Overhaul and Calibration Centre and NAFTRAC training of 453 aircraft engineering personnel on 13 aircraft types in the Nigerian Air Force. These are very remarkable as it added to the quality and dynamics to determine the contextual situational successes of the Nigerian Air Force. Significantly, these strides boosted the serviceability of Nigerian Air Force platforms in support and sustenance of counterterrorism and counterinsurgency operations in Operations HADARIN DAJI, THUNDER STRIKE, HADIN KAI and GAMA AIKI among others with tremendous victories and dominance. It is for this reason that we see many repentant terrorists.

Welfare

The Chief of Air Staff has performed so credibly with flying colours in so many areas of the service that he commands. He has boasted personnel welfare in different ways. In the last one year, the Chief of Air Staff renovated/remodelled and constructed new blocks of classrooms and hostel accommodation in existing Nigerian Air Force schools across the country. He engaged in a massive construction and renovation of residential accommodation to reduce the accommodation shortages in Nigerian Air Force Bases nationwide. These achievements are as though the Chief of Air Staff has spent more than ten years to accomplish these. This for this study is true and genuine Patriotic Citizenship.

Nigerian Air Force Civil Schools

The achievements of the Chief of Air Staff are numerous and outstanding within such a short time. The theoretical analysis on how this great leader could attain this within such a short period of time could be seen in the strain and differential theories. The strain schools believe that the mainstream of human culture is saturated with the dreams of opportunity, freedom and prosperity. According to Merton (1957) the dreams of self –actualization prompted some people into powerful socio-cultural and psychological motivation. Merton saw this as a dichotomy between what a society is expected from its citizens and what the citizens actually do. This invariably means that if the social structure of opportunities in a society is unequal and mischief prevent majority from realising their dreams some people will prefer to turn to illegitimate means of realizing their dreams. These theories identify needs, deprivation and frustration as the cause of conflict, violent acts and criminality. It therefore, juxtaposes that when a leader does what is highly unexpected within such a limited time, the Patriotic Citizenship of those who could not perform even with enough resources is doubtful.

The Chief of Air Staff's determination to improve the poor welfare package of temporary teaching staff in Nigerian Air Force Schools nationwide, which has been left unattended to by successive administrations is what this study commends strongly. Air Marshal Amao approved a 50 per cent upward review of salaries of all temporary teachers in Nigerian Air Force primary and secondary schools nationwide. The increment cuts across both Bachelor of Science (BSc) and National Certificate of Education(NCE) certificate holders. This has to a great extent increased the morale of the teachers. It has also improved their standards of living and created an impetus for better service delivery. Significantly, the pupils of Air Force Military School, (AFMS) and Air Force Girls Military School both located in Jos got a boost in their feeding ration allowance from N600 to N1,000.

This has gone a long way to improve their nutrition and in a way encouraged Patriotic Citizenship.

The Chief of Air Staff's priority and zeal to encourage qualitative education achieved the desired effect as students of Nigerian Air Force schools such as Air Force Military School, Jos, Air Force Girls Comprehensive School, Abuja, Air Force Secondary Schools, Ikeja and Shasha, Air Force Comprehensive Schools, Yola and Enugu respectively performed creditably in all their WASC/NECO exams with five credits including English and Mathematics respectively. Some of the benefits of the encouraged excellence in Nigerian Air Force are as enumerated below:

a. Master Edeani Izuchukwu, a student of Air Force Comprehensive School, Agbani, Enugu State emerged winner of the National Science Competitive Examination where he was awarded "774 Young Nigerian Scientists Presidential Award" by the Vice President, Professor Yemi Osinbajo.
b. Miss Feyisola Bolarinwa, a student of Air Force Girls Military School, Jos won the Bronze Award at the Queen's Commonwealth Essay Competition conducted by the Royal Commonwealth Society.

These are commendable outputs that the amiable leadership of the CAS has brought to bear on the entire community and family of the NAF. This study will wish that successive regimes will emulate this for posterity.

Office of the Ombudsman and the Directorate of Veterans Affairs Establishment

Another complimentary feat of the Chief of the Air Staff was the establishment of the above office. Thus, in approving the establishment of the Office of the Ombudsman, Air Marshal Oladayo Amao, took cognizance of the need to provide an avenue for those outside the

Service as well as Nigerian Air Force serving personnel to express their grievances against the Service for immediate resolution. This is the first of its kind in the military. Thus, the Nigerian Air Force personnel and those outside the service have the opportunity to channel their complaints and grievances against the service or its personnel. This is known as the Office of the Ombudsman and the Directorate of Veterans Affairs (DVA).

It is pertinent to note that that since the establishment of the Nigerian Air Force, its personnel have relied mostly on the provisions of the Executive Regulations in channeling their complaints for redress while in some cases, complaints were referred first to immediate superiors even when such complaints are against such superior officers. This is very important as justice could be attained with the new establishment.

The Directorate of Veteran Affairs will stimulate better welfare packages for Nigerian Air Force veterans and their families. The Directorate is charged with the responsibilities of interfacing with similar structures in sister Services towards harnessing necessary benefits for Nigerian Air Force retirees under existing Federal Government programmes for veterans within the spheres of the Military Pension Board.

Nigerian Air Force Telemedicine Portal

The former Chief of Air Staff has achieved another tremendous feat with the establishment of the Nigerian Air Force Telemedicine Portal. This in line with the Chief of Air Staff's vision to "enhance and sustain critical airpower capabilities required for joint force employment in pursuit of national security imperatives." It was in the interest of the service that the Chief of Air Staff sought to reduce the huge foreign exchange expended on medical tourism. Additionally, the challenge of COVID-19 pandemic and other likely viruses have drastically reduced physical contact between patient and doctors. It is for this reasons that the Chief of Air Staff approved the setting up of a Nigerian Air Force Telemedicine portal. This is the first of its kind in the military. The portal bridges the geographical barriers between patient and healthcare provider to access efficient and affordable healthcare services without being physically involved. It is also fast and efficient.

Another mile stone achievement is that the West African College of Physicians granted approval to the Nigerian Air Force to conduct Residency Training Programme for doctors in Family Medicine at the 661 Nigerian Air Force Hospital, Ikeja. This remarkable achievement came 18 years after the hospital was granted approval to train house officers by the Medical and Dental Council of Nigeria. This study is of the view that quality leadership could be attained more through military discipline, values and cultural ethics of high repute.

Thus, the hospital becomes the first and only hospital in the Nigerian Air Force accredited to train postgraduate medical doctors. It is heartwarming to also state that the laboratory of the same hospital equally won an award of International Organisation for Standardisation (ISO) 15189:2012 accreditation certificate for quality management systems and excellent service delivery. There cannot be a better word to describe this than to state here that this is true Patrotic Citizenship that the Nigerian State desires.

Research and Development in the Nigerian Air Force

There has been tremendous effort in the area of research and development. Nigerian Air Force has invested substantially in R&D to develop unprecedented capacity to surmount current and emerging security challenges while also enhancing its operational viability. These whole lots of achievements can only be borne out of a sincere willingness to achieve. In a country that is beset with public servants unaccountable to the lots of government funds that are being looted with impunity, these are exceptional strides that must be emulated.

The research feats were achieved through the Air Force Research and Development Centre. Some of the inventions included the refurbishment of unserviceable rocket launchers and BMGs back loaded from operations, test firing of locally produced 18-tube rocket launchers for A-jet aircraft and the production and deployment of 30.1mm rocket to 271 Nigerian Air Force Detachment, Birnin-Gwari for operational usage. Other achievements are the adaptation of 6-tube 68mm SNEB Rocket launcher on Agusta 109 Power Helicopter for improved fire power, reconfiguration of non-compatible DEFA Gun electrical flanges, installation of Geisha 23mm pintle mount with electrical firing system and the conversion of PUS 38DM to intervalometer. All these have helped the transform the operational capabilities of the Nigerian Air Force.

Infrastructural Development in Nigerian Air Force

This very key to human development and existence. One of the laudable efforts by the Chief of Air Staff is the availability of key infrastructures such as accommodation, roads and water in Nigerian Air Force Bases nationwide. This has in turn enhanced the morale of troops. It also has positive implications on Nigerian Air Force operational output as this leadership has ensured that special attention is given for the provision of basic needs in all Nigerian Air Force bases.

It is important to state here that over 15.41 kilometres of roads have been rehabilitated in Nigerian Air Force bases across the country. Some of these include the rehabilitation of selected road networks and asphalt resurfacing of 1600m road network at Nigerian Air Force Bases in Makurdi and Lagos, the rehabilitation of 781m link road from Officer's Quarters to NAFOM at Nigerian Air Force Base Kaduna.

There is also the construction of new road networks such as the flexible road from Bauchi Road to flight line at Nigerian Air Force Base Gombe, construction of link road from Headquarters Air Component to old runway. Additionally, another taxiway at 105 Composite Group Maiduguri and the construction of 1 km flexible road at AFRDC Osogbo. There is also the construction of additional link road to Military Apron at Nigerian Air Force Base Gombe as well as the construction of link road to Hangar at Nigerian Air Force Base Bauchi. In all, a total of about 7.5Km of new roads were constructed. It is worthy to note here that these exceptional achievements are commendable and should be documented for posterity. There are also over 100 blocks of different types of living accommodation at various levels of completion in Nigerian Air Force Bases nationwide.

Nigerian Air Force Paperless Process Automation Solution

This is another significant project that was conceived and approved for implementation under the quality leadership of Air Marshal Amao. This initiative which is currently close to completion is the first of its kind in the military and will be the first in any part of the country. It became necessary having observed Nigerian Air Force's overdependence on paper in its daily correspondences. This, the Chief of Air Staff sees as having negative environmental impact and makes it tedious to retrieve or track down specific documents. This invariably means that with the implementation of the paperless solution, less military vital secrets and other classified documents that are not shredded cannot be found elsewhere. Consequently, less time will be spent on clerical works to speed up document processing. Paper consumption will be drastically reduced. This will, help the environment.

Conclusion

With all these significant accomplishments by the former Chief of Air Staff, it is simply amazing that one would consider Air Marshal Oladayo Amao as outstanding in his sense of duty and commitment to the growth and development of the Nigerian Air Force. This is

Patriotic Citizenship which this study seeks to bring to bear to the psychology of building a virile and strong nation. The Chief of Air Staff was committed to transforming the Nigerian Air Force into a model fighting force that will operate seamlessly with the sister services and other security agencies to ensure security, stability, and prosperity of the nation. This study is also of the view that democratization in Africa is directly and could either be positively or negatively be correlated with conflict/ management. Some of these conflicts could lead to multiples of violent conflicts that could affect the true nature of Patriotic Citizenship. The study commends the immediate past Chief of Defence Staff, Gen LEO Irabor, the first Chief of Chief of Defence Staff Gen AG Olonisakin, former Chief of Army Staff, Lt Gen Tukur Burattai, Lt Gen Faruk Yahaya, the former Chief of Naval Staff, Vice Admiral Ibok and Vice Admiral Gambo, the former Chief of Air Staff, Air Mrashall Sadiq and Air Marshal Oladayo Amao for the high standards of operational excellence and combat readiness in carrying out its statutory roles as assigned by the President, Commander-in-Chief of the Armed Forces of the Federal Republic of NAGigeria, President Muhammadu Buhari. The nation will never forget their Patriotic Citizenship and Service to the Nigerian State.

References

Bribena KE, Ngboawaji DN, Ilyasu A, (May, 2022) Technical Intelligence and Security Management within the Nigerian Territorial Waters: The Nigerian Navy Challenge.

Cordesman, "The lessons and Non lesson of the Air and Missiles War in Kosovo." (Centre for Strategic and International Studies, Washington DC. September, 1999), p 231.

Corps and Services: Nigerian Army/ Official Website

Etina KA (2020) The role of the military to national development in Nigeria.

Liberman, "Transforming National Defence for 21ˢᵗ Century," (Washington: DC 1999) p.97.

Library.navtrac.com.ng

JS Peters. The State and the Nigerian Military, Zanus Publishers, 2001, p. 138.

M Yahaya, "The NAF and Development of Air Power in Imobighe. T. (ed) Nigerian Defence and Security. Issues and option for policy. (Ibadan Macmillan 1987. P.84).

Nigerian Army Resource Centre. https://narc.org.ng

Pape RA (1996) Bombing to Win: Air Power and Coercion in War (Itaca, New York: Cornell University press 1999), p 22.

P.E Tyler, "US Says Early Air Attack Iraq Off guard." New York Times, January, 18, 1991.

Planning Research and Statistic (Ministry of Defence) https:/defence.gov.ng>prs

The Making of the Nigerian Navy (2004) A Publication of the Policy and Plans of the Nigerian Navy (p. 10). C & A Prints Nigeria Limited.

Training and Doctrine (TRADOC) Nigerian Army TRADOC Official Website.

Chapter

6

Military Service and the Invaluable Sacrifice to Patriotic Citizenship and Service

Introduction

The Nigerian Armed Forces is the pride of the Nigerian State. Many officers and men who joined the military with lots of hopes and aspirations have had to pay the supreme prize. This study is of the view that their sacrifice will not be in vain. Our country remains the most populous black rack and vibrant experts in human capital development. The Armed Forces have lost thousands of her men in both foreign operations as well as violent conflicts within the country. The figures differ from one service to the other. Suffice to state here that the military has contributed enormously more than any institution in the unity of the country. Such strides to develop and unite the country are at variant to the political elites and academia stand on nation building. Service to our country is not negotiable. Nigeria perhaps is one of the most deeply divided states in the world. This has made it easy for her citizens to derail from patriotism when there is an outcry of injustice based on ethnic and religious matters. It is therefore, very necessary for us to put the country first and see everyone the same with honour and respect irrespective of where they hail from. Kirk-Green (1969) affirms that there exist over 400 ethnic groups in Nigeria. These groups are further divided along class and religious lines making our country very unique and complex. The uniqueness of my country's structural composition according to, Onwuejeowu (1995:23) reasons "creates unique problems unknown to the experience of other people in the world."

This has made it very important for us to continually appreciate the works of our fallen heroes who laid down their lives in the course of protecting our nation from her adversaries as well as unpatriotic and criminal citizens. This study is also of the view that the children of these heroes can be given enough support especially as most of them could not have possibly been done with their university education. State governments as well as wealthy individuals can periodically show concern for such challenged families rather than only remember them on specific days of the year. In certain climes, those that paid the supreme prize for their nations are never forgotten. The state takes care of all the needs of the loved ones that they left behind.

Power of Service

There is nothing as useful as the pride of service. It makes the country very powerful and self-sufficient in a lot of things. The power of a collective service by the citizens of any nation will lead to the prosperity of its people. The contrary is the case for nations without the patriotic willingness to serve by its people. Such a state will inspite of its natural resources find it difficult to survive. Lotters of public funds who are at the helm of affairs will institutionalise corruption and wreck the state of its economic mainstay. This and other vices will create unending crimes that are supposedly known amid the loss of many lives. Investors will find it difficult to do business with such people. This will put the nation in serious problems and force her to borrow from the international financial agencies putting her further into catastrophic situations. Inflation will soar causing the citizens to groan in abject poverty and want.

This is the situation that Nigeria finds herself today. It is an unwillingness by many citizens to truly serve. Rather, crimes have become a sector of her economy where sponsors drain the state of the pride to protect its citizens while many shamelessly walk talk in the horrible events that trouble the land. There are too many unanswered questions about why the country found herself in this terrible mess. Excellent Service can affect the lives of everyone within that state. If the citizens are sick and tired of the blemishes, then some institutions of government will wake up and do the right thing.

The Late Colonel Mamman Ghaddafi turned his country Libya around by making it one of the riches in Africa. With the country's enormous wealth before the death of its leader, her citizens were self-sufficient in basic human needs. Those who are not ready to impact human lives have no business with governance. They could go into other forms of human endeavours rather than destroy the destiny of a people. If you give a passenger aircraft with over 300 passengers onboard the flight to a half-baked pilot, you have most probably sent everyone on board that flight to an untimely death. The collective destiny of a people could be destroyed by leaders who are not willing to serve.

Emergency of Terrorism and Banditry

If there is anything that could destroy the safety of a nation, it is the proliferation of crimes and criminals. The Fourth Republic brought a lot of problems to the economic and security sector of the country making some schools of thoughts already considering the Nigerian State as a failing one. The non-state actors seem to have caused a catastrophic blow on the country making it obvious that majority of her citizens have not truly served positively.

The emergence of terrorism and then much later banditry in Nigeria which was quite unexpected brought a new security dimension to the country which the military, police and other security agencies have to rise to the occasion. The threat to the National Security had subsequently changed. Let us look at the emergentist theory. It provides a deeper and intellectual explanation of a social phenomenon through its use. This has informed its choice in deepening the various variables that gave birth to its religious motive. The term emergent was first known as a term in 1875 by GH Lewes along term resultant in further deepening the distinction by Mill's between homeopathic and heteropathic laws. Thus, it has become the widely accepted origin of the concept of emergence.

The emergence of the Boko Haram and Bandits have changed the scope of military operations and engagements. It has also brought in another unorthodox type of security facet which have had to be dealt with holistically. The political undertones are obvious and damning. Although at the initial stage of the inception of the insurgency some people had cold feet towards it as they saw it like in the light of the categories of a geo-political zone militia such as the Odua People Congress (OPC), the Niger Delta militants and the MASSOB geo-political militant groups. The Boko Haram terrorist was initially assumed to be a Hausa – Fulani ethnic militia. Unfortunately, this assumption turned out to be wrong as the sect began to attack and kill many pious Muslims and inflict terrible havoc to those worshipping in the mosques.

The violence conflicts that characterize the emergence challenge is at variance with the indices that allowed their growth up to this level thereby, giving some wrong scholarly concepts about the military and other security agencies not being able to curb these dangerous trends.

Military Legacies and Nationbuilding

The military is the backbone of the country's democratic growth. Most of the political and developmental efforts were carried out by the military regimes. This study is not in support of military government. Unfortunately, the First Republic could not offer the Nigerian people the dividends of democracy. Rather, the period witnessed series of political violence and killings in different parts of the country. The Nigerian Armed Forces have no doubt left no stone unturned to see how it can continue to be the hope of the country by the persistence in helping to preserve the country's democracy at very trying times like this. The military government under President Olusegun Obasanjo opted for the Presidential System of government modeled after the United States of America to accommodate the 400 ethnic groups in the country. Unfortunately, the system is not yielding the desired results as politicians have not played the Patriotic Citizenship role that is expected of them.

The failure of the previous Republics was also the inability to truly to serve the nation properly. Rather than see an improvement in nationbuilding, there seem to be a defective willingness not to encourage unity and patriotism within the various ethnic groups due to political divide and disagreements. The election seasons are usually not good times for the country as insincerity clouds the expectations of the people. In the end, the people are worse divided than united with so much suspicions and disagreements. This study is of the view that we can do away with these challenges.

Creation of an Agency With Support From Wealthy Nigerians for Widows, Incapacitated Ones and the Military Personnel that Died in Active Service

The military is a unique institution with Patriotic Citizenship in true display. It could be locally said that madness is not for kids. This simply put is that it is not easy for a normal person to face the type of fire power that the soldiers see in combat or during certain ambush and surprise attacks. Those that carry arms especially in the military have already put their lives at risk. Although life itself is filled with many unknown catastrophes, casualties and death is more pronounced during arms conflicts. Some military personnel have life time injurious that have kept them in military hospitals for life at

Maiduguri and Lagos respectively. They undergo treatments and are under the care of the hospitals. Although the military is responsible for their upkeep, such persons could also be shown compassion from wealthy persons as their condition is very pathetic. Some of them had these injuries during the ECOMOG Operations in Liberia and Sierra Leone. The military operations in the North East also have personnels who were casualties and have remained in the military hospital for many years. Their sacrifice is Patriotic Citizenship and true service to the Nigerian State.

Ensuring Robust Payment of Military Pension

The government of President Muhammadu Buhari did a lot to improve the payment of military veterans. This has reduced the mortality rate among retired military personnel. In the past the payment of veterans was very epileptic. Many who could not afford medical bills died in their numbers. Unfortunately, recently it has become extremely difficult to come to terms with some unusual realities. It has been observed that there is high level of compromise and corruption by some staff in charge of overseeing the functionality of the day to day running of certain payment. This has made it difficult for veteran to celebrate sallah. This is not encouraging for those who laid down their lives for the service of the nation. Those sabotaging their payment do not patriotic.

Conclusion

It is of great necessity to have a functional military with the necessary welfare that encourages both those in active service and the ones that are retired. We all feel safer knowing that the soldiers are out there keeping the watch for our safety. For non combat actors or civilians in this great country, it can be easy to forget the value and sacrifices the military has made over the years by keeping the country safe from insurgents and other societal criminals. This sacrifice has continued in the combat zones and many other places. For these sacrifices, the military should be valued and appreciated.

Our words and actions especially support should be to encourage the military not what we sometimes do to discourage them. There should be no middle ground. The words spoken into our lives have a tremendous amount of impact on our performance. We should encourage the military as they continue to do exploits. The wounded, widows and other challenged military personnel could be supported by the wealthy in the society. This will go a long way to encourage them to truly serve and improve Patriotic Citizenship.

References

Biekart, K. (2015). Guillermo O'Donnell's 'Thoughtful wishing' about democracy and regime change. Development and Change, 46(4), 913–933. https://doi.org/10.1111/dech.12167 [Crossref], [Web of Science ®], [Google Scholar]

Bueno de Mesquita, B, Smith, A, Siverson, R, M, & Morrow, J, D. (2003). The Logic of Political Survival.

Cawthra, G., & Luckham, H. (2003). Governing insecurity: Democratic control of the military and security establishment in transitional democracies. Zed Books. [Google Scholar]

Ferguson, P. A. (2004, June). Breaking up is hard to do: Incorporating democratic uncertainty into rational choice accounts of democratic breakdown [Paper presentation]. The Annual General Meetings of the Canadian Political Science Association. Winnipeg, Manitoba. Retrieved October 25, 2020, from https://www.cpsa-acsp.ca/papers-2004/Ferguson,%20Peter.pdf [Google Scholar]

Mainwaring, S., & Perez-Linan, A. (2013). Democratic breakdown and survival. *Journal of Democracy*, 24(2), 122–137. https://doi.org/10.1353/jod.2013.0037 [Crossref], [Web of Science ®], [Google Scholar]

Power, T. P., & Power, N. (1988). Issues in the consolidation of democracy in Latin America and Southern Europe in comparative perspective - A rapporteurs' report. *Working Paper No. 113*. Kellogg Institute series. [Google Scholar]

Wintrobe, J. (1998). The political economy of dictarship. Constitutional Political Economy, 10, 203–205.

Chapter

7

Leadership and Vision

Introduction

Patriotic Citizenship in soldering has a unique leadership trait based on honour and discipline. This is because the job in most climes puts the soldier in very critical situations with sometimes having to pay the supreme prize. In some countries the citizens must go through some military compulsory service for a short period to inculcate the oneness of the state to such citizens at an early stage in life. Leadership plays a very important role in the growth of the military and any organization as well as nations across the world. A great leader can establish very cordial and strong relationship with his subordinates or followers and motivate them to achieve the goals of their organizations with excellence. Where a leader especially in the military is focused and well respected, his soldiers can die for him and will follow him to the most dreaded military battle. In the military, every commander is trained to possess certain qualities that makes them stand outstanding even after military service. This is not to say that other organizations do not possess the qualities that this book tries to buttress, but to completely align to any good quality that are expressed in human followership. Let us look these qualities one after the other:

a. A leader is one who can think and does not merely follow the multitude.
b. A leader influences the behavior of his subordinates and others.
c. A leader has a powerful intellect and they impact their subordinates' to work hard.
d. A good leader should be morally upright.
e. A good leader listens to his people and will communicate well with them.
f. The leader must be selfless and filled with passion for his people especially the poor.
g. He/She must be able to encourage team work among those at the helm of affairs.
h. A good leader must have the quality of calmness.
i. A good leader must be kind hearted but firm.

Conceptual Discourse: Two key word will be discussed in this study. These are Leadership and vision. They will be conceptualized to show their importance for this study.

Leadership

According to Mc Kinsey, leadership is a set of behaviours used to help people align their collective direction, to execute strategic plans and to continually renew. This makes a lot of sense in the zeal to foster Patriotic Citizenship. For Wikipedia, Leadership, both as a research area and as a practical skill, encompasses the ability of an individual, group or organization to "lead," influence or guide other individuals, teams, or entire organizations. According to Forbs, the word "leadership" often gets viewed as a contested term. Leadership is a process of social influence, which maximizes the efforts of others, towards the achievement of a goal. These definitions are very helpful for this study as they colectively addressed the issue. However, in a simplistic take on this study, leadership is at all levels of human activities, the ability to be selfless, sincere and devoted to the commitment of Patriotic

Citizenship, from the family, ward, village, Local Government and State. In Nigeria's context, the federal powers, institutitions, local and national companies as well as industries are for the overall benefit and goodwill of the country. The list includes the owners of little and big enterprises. If a group of people run a man's company or that of the State down on account of selfish reasons, or run their local governments down, they do not have Patriotic Citizenship.

Vision

According to Wikipedia, a vision is something seen in a dream, trance or religious ecstasy, especially a supernatural appearance that usually conveys a revelation. For Macmillan dictionary, vison is uncountable the ability about and plan for the future, using intelligence and imagination especially in politics and business. In essence, the success of a government rests on its ability to define a vision for the country that reflects an electoral government.

The Realities of the Situation of Leadership and Patriotic Citizenship in Africa

Right from the end of colonialism in Africa, the continent seems to be pestered with the struggle for viable leadership that can turn around the fortune of its people. While some states have done well in meeting the challenges of the post-colonial era some have not. Unfortunately, a few sit-tight leaders have turned themselves to life Presidents. This is not the way for Patriotic Citizenship.

According to by Corinne Momal-Vanian:

> "Politics is the art of making possible what is necessary."

However, this does apply to many states in Africa. Political leadership is indeed the missing link between the many challenges that African states face on one hand and other numerous ones on the other hand. These are the wealth of knowledge and technical solutions available on the other. These without doubt goes a long way to influence; the well-being and good living standards of societies and citizens' confidence in governments. Unfortunately, what we have in Africa are mostly leaders who are unable to solve the increasing arms conflicts, growing ethnicity and hardships, economic obscurity, neo- colonial influence, geo-political shifts, climate change challenges such as flood, pandemic emergencies etc.

In many countries across the world especially in Africa, the voters are disillusioned with democracy. The people do not seem to be happy with the hardship that they go through. Their trust in politicians and governments is at all times low. Thus, the latest edition of the Democracy Perception Index shows that governments are simply not living up to the expectations of their citizens. This is so because, the standard of living is continually very high. This study is of the view that though training in key areas of policy and skills are important, political leadership should be more about empathy, vision and integrity.

Politicians should do the needful in embracing Patriotic Citizenship and Service. A key point for citizen engagement should be developing and sharing positive narratives on Patriotic Citizenship and nation first philosophies. Then this could lead to discussions on democracy and how and why citizens should get involved. There is the need to discuss on the hardship in the land as well as the palliatives efforts as well as other challenges such as inflation and unemployment. These will bring progress and create a strong nation with love.

Theories for Political Leadership

The agreement on the relevance of political leadership theory and practice seems to have some deficit in literature as regards viable approaches that could assist certain factors and suitable personality characteristics. It is important to note that suggested models for political leadership are mostly untested. This makes the results unreliable. This study proposes the development of a conceptual framework which could be helpful to come up with a model for political leadership. This is because there are too many theories which do not meet up with the variables and hypothesis expected in the end. Interestingly, two themes were accepted.

Two themes and four processes of political leadership were acknowledged. It was easier to select from them. Thus, a conceptual framework for political leadership theory and practice was developed. Significantly, the framework was able to come up with two components of political leadership theory and practice. It also pointed out set of relationships. Thus, the framework permits individual themes to occur repeatedly through the political leadership field. The results of the study can serve as a primary model for developing an extended understanding of the theory and practice of political leadership. This can further be used in other disciplines such as political science, economics, sociology, and psychology. It could serve as a guide in determining inter-relational dynamics in political leadership patterns, behaviors, and character traits of leaders in future studies. This is very important as it helps this study to come up with the adequate variable that could be used for leadership and Patriotic Citizenship.

It is important to state here that leadership can be seen in two varied ways. The difference between a political leader and a politician is not arguable (Joensuu & Niiranen, 2018). However, as stated by (Teles, 2012), while the political leader possesses both the passion and responsibility, the politician is normally associated with achieving political goals without necessarily aligning means, ends, and consequences. In many cases, some of the goals and mandates are never accomplished with no consequences. This explains why some leadership will make certain erroneous decisions close to the end of their governments.

Significantly, the two set of leaders perform two different functions. Even though the two leaders may hold the same or similar offices, they both have separate intentions from their roles based on approaches to executing mandates and not on functions. This invariably portends that the superiority of leading as against accomplishing in a political setting is different.

Political leadership was further reiterated that political leadership is a game-changer (Teles, 2012). He added that many social outcomes are heavily dependent on it. The domineering role of political leadership has been re-emphasized severally. There are also enough literature that supports this assertion, (Gane, 1997; Yukl, 2002; Peele, 2005). This study is of the view that political ledership is very important as it helps to promote peace in the land. All contending issues are addressed amicably without conflicts. For King et al, political leadership is an important and indispensable element to societal advancement and development (King et al.,2015). This is very significant for the economic growth and prosperity of the people. According to Harriss, (2000) the absence of ineffective political leadership systems and structures have been known to create festering vacuum where disorder, chaos and trepidation thrive.

Essence of Good Leadership

The essence of any form of authority that has to do with leading the government is in the hands of the elected political office holders or the representatives that are chosen by the citizens in a democratic process known as elections. This is different from Authoritarian, Dictatorship or Kakistocracy systems of government. In the true context, Democracy has no connotation if there is no feeling of love and unity among the people. The sense of unity and Patriotic Citizenship must be the corner stone in the oneness of the society. There must be a feeling among the people who are known to be the children of the same nation or what is said to be same motherland. This is what the great Late Sonny Okosun called fatherland. It depicts the same thing. Significantly, democracy does not mean only political democracy. It also portrays social and economic democracy. Thus, a Patriotic Citizenship leadership in a good democratic setting will do well for the people rather than create ethnic divide as it's the case with tribal leaders.

Patriotic Citizenship, the family and leadership

In this context, this study intends to drive the spirit of nationhood as an attitude that should have its root from the family. This is very important. There is the adage that states that the behaviour of a child is determined by that child's upbringing. Parents that train their children to use derogatory words on other tribes such as does not seem to be promoting Patriotic Citizenship. In most families in the past, parents teach the children the values of the Nigerian State. These includes the ability to be able to recite the National Anthem, the National Pledge and many other important things, such as the ability to know the name of the president and other important personalities at the federal level, all the governors in the country, the number of local government, states etc. Today, this is not the case. It is therefore, difficult to have our children embrace Patriotic Citizenship.

The Essential Variables of Political Leadership

Political leadership is very interesting as it makes room for so many alternatives towards ensuring the progress of the state and improvement in the standard of living. These usually comes from leaders that are willing to do well for the state. So many excesses take place that are not detected until the end of that particular government. Modern democracies have welfare packages that assist citizens in all aspects of life. The citizens also participate in a wide range of decision making that affects them through their representatives.

It is important to state here that political leadership has four variables. These are:

    a. Political Promise
    b. Political Mandate
    c. Political Representation

d. Political Causation

Political Promise

One of the political process in a democratic system is the various promises that politicians make to the electorates during campaigns. These are to entice the voters to cast their votes for them. Most of the promises are towards the development of the state. However, these promises are hardly met in some cases especially in Africa where you have sit-tight democratic governments.

Political Mandate

This is the second step in an electoral process. According to (Morrell and Hartley, 2006), political mandate is officially granted by an electorate to govern in accordance with stated policies. For (Torfing and Sorensen, 2019), the ability of poitical leaders to effectively interact with the public is also an essential activity that transforms traditional understanding of democratic mandate. It is important to state that some ailing democracies lack any form of mandate. At the sametime, the electorate do not have the political education and awareness to demand for certain rights embedded in a democratic constitution. So, they have little or no contribution to their system of government. This was the case with the former Sudanese government.

Political Representation

This variable states that the representative process involves development or increase in the relationship between two parties with certain rights and responsibilities among key players. Suffice to state that the two parties have multilevel rights and responsibilities that have recognisable beginning and end (Andonov et al., 2018; Traber et al. 2018; Conti et al., 2018). The Stanford Encyclopedia of Philosophy describes political representation as "the activity of making citizens' voices, opinions, and perspectives 'present' in public policy making process," and further outlined the process to include; 1) a representing party, which could be an individual, an organisation, a movement, or a state agency; 2) a represented party, which includes constituents or clients; 3) a represented interest, opinion, discourse, or perspective; 4) a political context within which the process of representation occurs; and 5) perspectives and interests that are left out. In another perspective, which is apt for this study, Powell Jr (2004) asserts that democratic representation requires that policy makers are supposed to meet the aspirations of the people they represent. If the people that are represented in a democratic dispensation are well catered for, they will embrace Patriotic Citizenship. On the contrary if the political office holders do not embrace the unity that is derived from statehood, the objectives of Patriotic Citizenship will not be upheld.

Political Causation

The fourth on the list for this study is very important. It is the analysis of cause and effect. This invariably means that politicians on the side of Patriotic Citizenship engage in roles in order to achieve political goals and objectives. These include welfare packages such as the empowerment of the underprivileged, improving the social contract law by ensuring the safety of the people. Improving the education of the youth through grant as implemented by the government of President Bola Ahmed Tinubu and the welfare packages granted by developed democracies is what this variable looks at. The living standard of the common man could be better if Patriotic Citizenship is embraced by leadership at all levels.

Conclusion

Leadership and Vision are two very important variables in a democratic government. Leadership can take a country to paradise or damnation. Countries with very strong leadership figures have achieved so much than those who do not possess leadership qualities. Mahatma Gandhi's leadership was superb. He turned India around with great things and development strides. His aim was always clearly defined, his lead was unequivocal and full of purpose. Political leadership studies can be very interesting as there are many literatures on the subject. However, it is important that political leadership theory and practice should not be confused with an on the spot overview of intended political goals which might not be accomplished eventually. Vision helps in fulfilling political goals with zeal. This study is of the view that leadership without vision is very dangerous for any state. Therefore, Patriotic Citizenship should be passionately handled by political office holders.

References

Bennister, M., Worthy, B., & Hart, P. T. (Eds.) (2017). The Leadership Capital Index: A New Perspective on Political Leadership. Oxford, England: Oxford University Press.https://doi.org/10.1093/oso/9780198783848.001.0001

Butcher, D. & Clarke, M. (2006). Political leadership in democracies: some lessons for business? Management Decision, 44 (8), pp. 985-1001.

Burns, J. M. (1978) Leadership. New York, YK: Harper & Row.

Butcher, D., & Clarke, M. (2006). Political Leadership in Democracies: Some Lessons for Business? Management Decision, 44, 985-1001. https://doi.org/10.1108/00251740610690577

Conti, N., Hutter, S., & Nanou, K. (2018). Party Competition and Political Representation in Crisis: An Introductory Note. Party politics, 24, 3-9. https://doi.org/10.1177/1354068817740758

Cornell, C., & Malcomson, P. (2016). Prudence and Glory: Machiavelli on Political Leadership. In J. Masciulli, M. A. Molchanov, & W. A. Knight (Eds.), The Ashgate Research Companion to Political Leadership (pp. 51-64). Farnham and Burlington, VT: Ashgate.

Gandhi, M. K. (1942). The Picture of Village Swaraj. The Harijan, 28-7-42.

Garfield, Z. H., von Rueden, C., & Hagen, E. H. (2019). The Evolutionary Anthropology of Political Leadership. The Leadership Quarterly, 30, 59-80.https://doi.org/10.1016/j.leaqua.2018.09.001

Selznick, P. (1957). Leadership in Administration. New York, 22-24.

Tead, O. (1936). The Art of Leadership. Mc-Graw Hill, New York, 20.

Chapter

8

The Pursuit for Patriotic Citizenship and a Genuine Democratic Best Practice for Nigeria

Introduction

Most countries across the world are in a new trend where they try to embrace democracy and abandon an old so called undemocratic practice be it authoritarian or military government. Thus, Samuel Huntington (1999), in his book titled the Third Wave stated that the world is now in the midst of a third wave of democratic expansion. This is a drive that is very strong. According to him, a wave of democratization is a group of transitions from non-democratic to democratic regimes that occur within a specified period of time. He argued that the first wave dates back to 1828 with the expansion of democratic suffrage in the United States. Samuel Huntington stated that the second wave, which is a shorter democratic wave began with the allied victory in World War 2. Importantly, the second got to 1962. This was a period that some colonies which included a number of Latin American and quite a number of newly independent former British colonies got their liberations and independence. The third wave began around the 1970s. At this time, there was a global phenomenon especially in the 1980s and 1990s, a remarkable series of changes in the world system. Suddenly, the cold war ended with a renewed zeal for democratization. It was at this time that many African countries were liberated from undemocratic governments. It was during this period that some countries in Africa got their independence. An example is South Africa under the apartheid regime. Ironically too, Nigeria was at the forefront of liberation struggles.

-Conceptual Clarifications

The concepts that are central to this study are: Patriotic, Citizenship, Democratic and Best Practice.

Patriotic

To be patriotic is the feeling of attachment and commitment to a country, nation or political community. Significantly, patriotism which is the love of country and nationalism which is loyalty to one's nation are most often taken to be synonymous. However, patriotism dates back to 2,000 years' prior the rise of nationalism in the 19th century.

It is important to state here that Greek and especially Roman antiquity provide the roots for a political patriotism that conceives of loyalty to the patria as loyalty to a political conception of the republic. This is associated with the love of law and common liberty. It is the search for common good and the duty to behave justly to one's country. This is the same with the classical Roman meaning of Patria. In the context of the Italian City Republics of the 15th century, Patria stands for the common liberty of the city, which can only be safeguarded by the citizen's civil spirit. Thus, for Niccolò Machiavelli, the love of common liberty enabled citizens to see their private and particular interests as part of the common good and helped them to resist corruption and tyranny. Significantly, while this love of the city is typically intermixed with pride in its military strength and cultural superiority, it is the political institutions and way of life of the city that form the distinctive main point of this kind of patriotic affection. To love the city is to be willing to sacrifice one's own good. This could include one's life, for the protection of common liberty. Patriotism is therefore, broader than we think.

Citizenship

This has earlier been discussed in this book. However, the concept is vague as it means differently depending on the clime or place. In its simplest term, citizenship is a legal status. That means a person has a right to live in a state and that state cannot refuse them entry or deport them. This legal status may be conferred at birth, or, in some states, obtained through 'naturalisation.' In wealthy liberal democratic states, citizenship also brings with it rights to vote, rights to welfare, education or health care etc. In this official sense, citizenship acquisition for oneself or one's children is seen as principally related to migrants. This is with reference to the western world and her democracies. For instance, a child born in the country Nigeria of his parents or either of them is a Nigerian.

However, it is important to note that citizenship does not only concern the migrants, but is more generally about individuals' relations to the state and to each other. Liberal 'republican' positions in particular have emphasised the relation between citizenship and political participation such as voting, engagement in civil society and other forms of political mobilisation. Additionally, this is also a legal status such that citizenship can also indicate a subjective feeling of identity and social relations of reciprocity and responsibility. Occasionally, these can be described in words like 'loyalty', 'values', 'belonging' or 'shared cultural heritage.' This also points to the complex and often assumed relation between citizenship and belonging to 'the nation.'

It is necessary to state here that the British debate on immigration and citizenship occurred within a context of more than a decade of policies and reviews on citizenship. In 1979, when the Labour government came to power, it strongly emphasized 'active citizenship.' This was an attempt to transform citizens from what was perceived as 'passive recipients of public services' to actively engaged participants in public life (Mayo and Rooke 2006).

Then, in 1998 a policy review of citizenship education in England was conducted by Sir Bernard Crick. In September 2002, following its recommendation, citizenship education was introduced as a statutory subject in English secondary schools. There has been nothing like this in most parts of Africa. Also in 2002 The Advisory Board on Naturalisation and Integration (ABNII) was established. It was chaired by Sir Bernard Crick, to develop proposals for language and citizenship courses and tests for applicants to British citizenship. This took place against the background of a number of disturbances in towns in Northern England, including Bradford, in 2001, which gave rise to concerns about 'community cohesion' and a lack of 'shared values' (Home Office 2001a; Ryan 2010). The 'Life in the UK Advisory Group' situated its work within a much broader policy remit, including 'a wider citizenship agenda'.

In 2007, the then Prime Minister Gordon Brown requested a review of British citizenship to clarify the legal rights and responsibilities of different categories of citizenship and nationality, and the incentives for residents to become citizens. The 'Lord Goldsmith Citizenship Review' was also requested to 'explore the role of citizens and residents in civic society. This included voting, jury service and other forms of civil participation.'

Democratic

Democratic comes from the word, democracy. Therefore, democracy is a system of government that places absolute power to the people. It is government of the people for the people and by the people. It is a form of government that empowers the people to exercise political control, provide for separation of powers between the various organ of government, ensure the protection natural rights as well as civil liberties.

It is a system of government that empowers the people to exercise political control. The system is differently practiced from one country to another. It makes provision for the separation of powers as well as the rule of law. It also provides for certain freedom and civil liberties. Such as freedom of speech, freedom of association etc. There are different types of democracies. These are the parliamentary system, the presidential, pluralist, constitutional system and socialist democracies.

Best Practice

A best practice simply means a method or technique that has been generally accepted worldwide as superior to other known alternatives because it often produces results. This is because it is often seen to produce results that are superior to those achieved by other means, or because it has become a standard way of doing things. It is a standard way of complying with legal or ethical requirements. Best practices are used to maintain quality as an alternative to mandatory legislated standards and can be based on self-assessment or standard. Best practice is a feature of accredited requite standard even in the political space. It is the standard for yielding the dividends of democracy. It is the standard where transparency and accountability is the order of the day for good governance. Where this lacking, it is only observing a wrong system of value.

The Travail of Nigeria's Democracies in the Fourth Republic

The Nigerian State is beset with numerous problems which she has been carrying for so many years after her independence. Many of these challenges were erroneously blamed on the military intervention in power rather than the political and academic elites who were also part of the policy making process for the running of the country during military regimes. Although the constitution during the periods were suspended, there were remarkable achievements which have been difficult to accomplish in the Fourth Republic. One of such was the vision for a new capital territory by the Murtala/Obasanjo regime and the construction of the Federal Capital Territory and the eventual relocation of the capital from Lagos to Abuja on 12 December 1991. While this study stands for Patriotic Citizenship in a Democratic Process that is driven by its sincere practices, it sees the achievement of the military in helping to transform the Nigerian State as truly nationalistic. Today, the Federal Capital Territory is Nigeria's pride with its beautiful landscape and world standard edifices. It is one of the most beautiful cities in the world while Lagos, the erstwhile capital retains the economic nerve of the country. With the new Dangote refinery, Lagos will be one of the most economically viable country in the world. Nigeria's intellectual and political elites have today seen the derogatory remarks on the military and its impact on the common people who also have sons and daughters of high learning standards. They made remarks such as, that the worst democratic regime is better than the best military regime. This for this study is simply put not marketable anymore and a wrong pro-democracy advocacy. Most Nigerians would reject this proposition outrightly. The truth is everywhere for the even the children and young adults to see. All the traumatized people who can hardly afford what to eat daily, families of those killed in the North East, the innocently kidnapped victims all over the country, thousands of unemployed graduates, the millions of poverty stricken families will agree that any performing system of governance will just do for the Nigerian State.

Nigerians have lived in diversity since independence. Although the country has gone through many tragedies and despair, the people have lived with hope for the next day. They lived in complacent like it had been since independence not seriously bothered about national political issues that could seriously affect them. All they crave for is peace and an environment to take care of themselves and their families. However, this is fast changing as the youth seem to have different rethink about their country. The EndSars riots across the country created a new form of change in police community relations. While quite a number of the young adults seem to be interested who rules over them, the majority of the typical Nigerians remain not really bothered. For (Nwankwo, 1997: xi) "The combination of an unconscionable leadership and an indifferent populace has created the haunting enigma that the community now is ......Strategic thinking and planning have been replaced by minor tactical survivalist devices that only ensure the passage of another day."

Certainly, it is this norm that seem to put Patriotic Citizenship on the downward slope. People do not want to believe in what they perceive to be untrue and lack merit. Patriotic Citizenship requires that a leader of the people will be able to stand out like a mentor to many citizens. He should be loved and motivated. However, since the beginning of the Fourth Republic in 1999, the essence of Patriotic Citizenship among the political leaders seems to be declining by the day. While some political office holders cannot recite the Nigerian National Anthem, many others aspire to hold appointments with little or nothing to offer. Their interest is not in what this study proffers but that of a pocket full of looted government funds while the masses suffer in abject poverty. Nigeria is said to be the poverty headquarters of the world, yet she is blessed with the richest mineral resources in the world.

It is of a truth that Nigeria is still groping in the dark in search of a viable Patriotic Citizenship that is driven by sincere leaders across board. While some institutions within the Nigerian State are weak, it is very certain that Patriotic Citizenship with accountability and service is lacking. During the First Republic, Nigeria had a regional system of government. This made it easy for the regions to be accountable to themselves. It is important to state here that under Chief Obafemi Awolowo, the speed of growth in the then Western Region was amazing. This was the same with other regions as each of them made giant strides in agriculture, technology, trade, economy and other developmental growth. We will not forget the groundnut pyramids in the north or the cocoa exploits in the west. There were numerous progress and growth.

With the collapse of the regional system of government, things began to change making the once giant of Africa, the ailing giant with the threat of disintegration but her military. Even the various successive governments knew that there was a problem of political growth of the country. With the inception of the Fourth Republic in 1999, several efforts have been made to help solve the Nigerian State challenge. Thus, several assumptions, creations and approaches have been suggested. Some have been put into practice with no form of remarkable output. In this Fourth Republic, Patriotic Citizenship has taken the backward stage as government actions are conceived through the lens of politics, not of patriotism. Thus, this study observed that in some instances, rather than ask if a policy or initiative is good for the Nigerian people, elected officials ask if it would look good politically. In the same vein, rather than find out how a policy might help Nigerians, officials ask how it would win them the next elections. This was evident during the recent change in the Naira. Many Nigerians died due to the hardship that it caused. This could have been avoided. This study will have its suggestion for a type of political system which could be useful for posterity.

Let us begin by looking at a few efforts made earlier. It is significant to state here that on 13 January, 1986, the federal military government under Gen Ibrahim Badamosi Babangida inaugurated a Political Bureau to conduct a national debate on the political future of Nigeria. This was shortly after the military junta overthrew the government of Gen Muhammadu Buhari that aborted the Second Republic. The key point and the specific terms of reference of the Political Bureau was the identification of "a basic philosophy of government which will determine goals and serve as a guide to the activities of government." The Bureau however, submitted a comprehensive report to the government on 27 March, 1987. Thereafter, nothing else was heard about the Bureau neither was any of its recommendations implemented.

In the same vein, the government of President Olusegun Obasanjo which began the Fourth Republic realized that there was the need to change the political setting of the country to something more viable. He initiated what he called, national reforms programmes. This one too did not see the light of the day. After his government came that of President Umaru Musa Yar'Adua with what he called "a seven-point agenda." Unfortunately, too, this agenda failed to transform the country. The Fourth Republic continued to suffer so many challenges as it failed to deliver the dividends of democracy. Nigerians with special qualifications and skills, like doctors, engineers, nurses, architects etc. began to leave the country for greener pastures. The government of President Goodluck Jonathan proposed a single term in office for the president and governors. While this looked very good and encouraging, many politicians frowned at it.

Additionally, President Goodluck Jonathan organized a national conference to discuss Nigeria's way forward politically. The recommendations of the 2014 conference which had about 492 delegates that represented a cross-section of Nigerians including the professional bodies was commended by many Nigerians. The conference which was headed by retired judge Idris Kutigi witnessed plenary sessions that lasted for weeks as the panels of discussants were broken into 20 committees that included Public Finance and Revenue sharing, devolution of powers, political restructuring and other critical issues of national value. The recommendations of the report of the conference were never implemented. Thus, there have been strident calls for political restructuring and devolution of powers by contending regional groups up to this day.

After the government of President Goodluck Jonathan, the country has witnessed a lots political, economic and social challenges which have further affected the unity of the country and wellbeing of the people. However, the resilience and peaceful nature of the people have kept the hopes of the masses on. It is important to state here that according to the vision 2020 report, the pillars of the Nigerian economy are extremely weak and the continued economic viability of the Nigerian State is perpetually at risk (cited in Kukah, 2012). It is therefore, extremely difficult for the country to sustain the current system of democratic governance. Poverty has increased with little or no daily meals for many families.

Our perception of democracy is a purely down-to-earth one. While it is easier for those in the developed world to understand intellectually what democracy means, the less developed world tends to ask what it can deliver to them. Nigerians evaluate democratic practice not in abstract or futuristic terms but in terms of its immediate benefits to their lives. This is absolutely necessary since the democracy that we practice is borrowed and not indigenous. This study is of the view that most of Africa's democracy has not lived up to their expected benefits. This is known by many people.

Federal System with a Strong Regional or Zones Powers

While the developed countries seem to be enjoying the gains of democracy, African States battle with evils that come with liberalism and a problematic democratic process. This study therefore, prescribes that Patriotic Citizenship will be better practiced through the Regional or Zonal System with a weak central government as the practical model for Nigeria. Additionally, the salaries and allowances of all political office holders should be realistic and the same with countries that have transparent democracies. This will make politics not attractive and a place for those who truly believe in Patriotic Citizenship and Service. Every region or zone should survive with what they generate locally, while the petro dollar oil revenue shared monthly should be known by the citizens. The local governments should be allowed to operate independently. The Exclusive, Concurrent and Residual Lists should be reviewed to meet the realities on ground. The Quota System should be properly practiced to the reflect equity and fairness. There should a strong clause in the constitution that enables each of the zones to produce a President of the Federal Republic of Nigeria.

Political Tyranny and Insensitivity

Where there is good governance and equity, the citizens will enjoy the dividends of democracy. However, where there is political rascality and insensitivity, wrong government policies will be made some of which might affect the common man adversely. In many cases, the people will suffer and die in their numbers especially with the high rate of poverty everywhere. In some countries in Africa, political insensitivity has taken the place of political excellence. Patriotic Citizenship stands for the truth, development, economic growth, honesty, good welfare package for the people and a secured environment. Where the latter is lacking, it could be compared to states that lack the virtues of true and sane democracies. It is like a state that mocks itself and leaks its own wounds. Foreign governments did not insist on good governance, either. Even when policies failed, assistance kept coming in form of loans, grants or aids. Increasingly, most Africans with Patriotic Citizenship drives are insisting that such conditions of assisting economically bankrupt states of Africa should be tied to policy performance. As Ake (1996:29) puts it, "if people are the end of development, then, their well-being is the supreme law of development. But the well-being of the people will only be the supreme law of development if they have only one way to ensure that social transformation is not dissociated from democracy."

However, rich a country might be, if the people are poor and in abject poverty, such a country's leadership needs a rethink on its Patriotic Citizenship. This is because most of its people especially the specialists and professionals that can afford to leave the country will do so with so much ease and seek the nationalities of other countries. Many

Nigerians are in countries that are less developed than the country. Patriotic Citizenship will provide leaders that are image makers internationally for the country. Today many Nigerians have serious ethnic dislike for each other. Rather, than have Patriotic Citizenship builders or unifiers, they work contrary to the goals and aspirations of a united Nigeria, creating confusions and causing distractions here and there even to the extent of cashing on ethnic or primordial interests as a ladder to achieve national goals (Tkhariale, 2012:3 1). This is very discouraging and a bad light to behold at a period where many nations are embracing new methods that make life easy for the common people.

Corruption and Democracy

The issue of corruption is a profound threat to all systems of government across the globe. This study chose to emphasize the need to have a transparent and accountable system where due process is strictly observed. In most African countries, corruption constitutes an important means by which individual wants and needs, especially in patronage-ridden personal regimes, can be satisfied. Such countries for example are North Korea and Russia where the head of state cannot be challenge as he has absolute powers. Although corruption is a general problem for all governments, governments of developing countries tend to exhibit the problem in a particularly remarkable way. In countries such as Nigeria, Ghana, Sierra Leone, Zaire, and the Central African Republic, Congo, The Gambia and Sudan, the problem is terrible. Thus, corruption is so widespread that it is viewed as a way of life. Making or receiving bribes in most African countries is considered a practical tactic to look after one's needs and interests. This in some instances could be far greater than the monthly salary. In Nigeria, the petrol dollar national cake and state governor's security vote are both means to loot the treasury. With an absence of effective structures with autonomy and strength to check corruption, the ruling elites of most African countries and their cohorts have engaged in outrageous levels of corruption. In Zaire, for example, corruption has been termed a structural fact, with as much as 60 percent of the annual budget misappropriated by the governing elite with no ounce of pity for the suffering masses that voted them into power.

Conclusion

This study looked at the search for Patriotic Citizenship and a Genuine Democratic Best Practice for Nigeria. This is in a bid to examine the rarity of Patriotic Citizenship in the Nigerian State. It argued that when one has the interest of the nation at heart, he will defend it with all the virtues that qualifies a good democratic dispensation. There will be economic and political transformation as witnessed in countries like South Africa and Rwanda to which Nigeria was better than in the past few decades. Hillary Clinton, during her stop-over visit to Nigeria in 2009, remarked that the poverty rate in Nigeria has gone up from 46 percent to 76 percent over the last 13 years. The people cannot be true citizens when they are hungry. This study is of the view that Patriotic Citizenship needs to be resuscitated among Nigerian citizenry and the need to search for a good system of government that can be credible and accepted by all Nigerians.

The study is of the view that Africa should have her model of political governance than the copied world systems that have not yielded the desired results. It wonders how the country can have a Patriotic Citizenship Service-oriented governance amid terrible ethnic divide as well as the spiteful succession of corruption which has produced the futuristic economic bankruptcy as well as political and social mess that now characterize the Nigerian State. The study therefore, submitted that the country should embark on an urgent need to rejuvenate Patriotic Citizenship and bring the country back to what it was in the past. It suggested a federal system of governance with zones capable of providing its own resources as well as local governments that are independent of the states to foster development.

References

Achebe, C (1983). The Trouble with Nigeria. Enugu: Fourth Dimension Publishers.

Ake, C. (1996). 'For Africa, the way forward', in The Guardian, 13 November. (1996). Democracy and Development in Africa. Tbadan: Spectrum Books Limited

Eboh, IIB. (2009) Great Giants of Wicked Purities: Authorhouse, London.

Hendriks, C. M. (2009). Deliberative Governance in the Context of Power. Policy and Society, 28, 173-184. https://doi.org/10.1016/j.polsoc.2009.08.004

Knight, W. A. (2016). Distinguishing and Unifying Visionary Leadership and Mechanical Management. In J. Masciulli, M. A. Molchanov, & W. A. Knight (Eds.), The Ashgate Research Companion to Political Leadership (pp. 135-148). Farnham and Burlington, VT: Ashgate.

King, A. S. N., Millanzi, M., Massoi, L., & Kyando, N. (2015). The Role of Political Leaders in Enhancing Peace and Tranquility: Thinking Big. International Journal of Managerial Studies and Research, 3, 84-90.

Kirvalidze, N., & Samnidze, N. (2016). Political Discourse as a Subject of Interdisciplinary Studies. Journal of Teaching and Education, 5, 161-170.

Kukah, M.H (2012), 'Nigeria as an Emerging Democracy: The Dilemma and the NIGERIA IN SEARCH OF DEMOCRATIC BEST PRACTICES" 187 promise Retneved from htp://www. leadership. ng/oga/articles/34644/ 2012/0971/nigeria emerging democracy dilemmna_and .pro

Hendriks, C. M. (2009). Deliberative Governance in the Context of Power. Policy and Society, 28, 173-184. https://doi.org/10.1016/j.polsoc.2009.08.004

King, A. S. N., Millanzi, M., Massoi, L., & Kyando, N. (2015). The Role of Political Leaders in Enhancing Peace and Tranquility: Thinking Big. International Journal of Managerial Studies and Research, 3, 84-90.

Kirvalidze, N., & Samnidze, N. (2016). Political Discourse as a Subject of Interdisciplinary Studies. Journal of Teaching and Education, 5, 161-170.

Chapter

9

The Threat of Electoral Violence to Patriotic Citizenship

Introduction

Democracy across the world has become the means through which credible and accountable leaders are elected to run the affairs of their people through free and fair credible elections. There are several forms of democratic governance in the world. While some earlier developed states chose their democracy to reflect their civilization and culture, many others only copy these democracies without the ability to have them properly implemented in their states. Human survival called for true citizens that crave to live together under a sovereignty that protect their lives and properties. Patriotic Citizenship therefore, requires that the people that inhabit the state must be totally loyal to it and not embark on any nefarious thing that could jeopardize the interest of the state. This is the challenge that we have in some African States where the people have lost interest in the democratic setting that have not yielded the dividends of democracy. Patriotic Citizenship desires that the people that own the state will work very hard to develop the state. Making any form of negative input by bringing the state down is not what this study stands for.

Violence has characterized the electoral process right from the country's independence 1st October 1960. This has made it difficult for the various tribes to co-exist without suspicion for different reasons. When it has to do with the various political parties seeking for political leadership of the country, the challenge is quite enormous. Unfortunately, what is expected to be a country with enormous human and natural resources has become a nation that is beset with lots of problems ranging from political, economic, social, security and even terrorism then banditry. This has made it difficult for the Nigerian State to truly excel.

The electoral process in the country has continued unabated with a surge in violent events involving political parties. This has seriously affected the Nigerian State. Violent conflicts have become a phenomenon with many people losing their lives. This is very disturbing as supporters of various political parties are attacked, killed or maimed during political activities. These partisan violence has escalated along ethnic and sectarian lines, resulting in multiple rounds of revenge killings and destruction of properties. Thus, that part of the former national anthem that states that "though tribe and tongue may differ in brotherhood we stand," only seems to be regarded as a mere statement.

Conceptual Clarification On Electoral Violence and its effect on Patriotic Citizenship

Electoral Violence will be conceptualized and the relationship and effect on Patriotic Citizenship established.

Electoral Violence

This is the unethical use of violence to truncate an electoral process for the political interest of a party. Unfortunately, elections held outside of consolidated democracies are often accompanied by substantial violence conflicts such as arson, destruction of properties, killings, maiming etc. In most cases, the indigenes of those communities try to ensure that their preferred political parties are voted for. The whole mess of it is that they threaten the non-indigenes living in their land with eviction if they do not play to the gallery. This is on the wrong path to true unity and Patriotic Citizenship that this study looks at.

Elections are held in many countries of the world as the government of the people through the ballot boxes seems the most accepted way to follow in the 21st Century. However, the increasing risk and danger posed by these elections leaves much to be desired. Violent conflicts readily rear their heads as it becomes a do or die affair. The electoral violence in the context of this study is like other forms of organized violence with foot soldiers of the political parties ready to unleash hate at those that are against their interest.

Effect of Electoral Violence on Patriotic Citizenship and Service

Patriotic Citizenship for this study is the total submission to the values and dignity of one's country. It is the essence of a citizen's pride for the country and the inward zeal to protect it from any form of wreck. Electoral violence on the other hand, is produced during electoral seasons. It reveals more than anytime, the fragility and soft skinned nature of the Nigerian State when it comes to unity and love for the Nigerian State. Nigeria's electoral history is awash with narratives of flawed, disputed and in some cases open truth that falls on the street. Thus, most elections turned out violent, resulting in numerous fatalities and destroying attempts at democratic consolidation since the beginning of the uninterrupted military intervention in the politics of Nigeria with the beginning of the Fourth Republic in 1999. The effect of these electoral violence is that it ended up further dividing the people into different unimaginable levels with many tribes and ethnic groups not believing in the Nigerian State. These divisions led to the school of thought that called the country's unity as the Nigerian Project. This study frowns at the word projects. However, what could be a more derogatory word than when Nigeria was said to be a "mere geographical expression?"

Therefore, for there to be unity of purpose and the identification of the Nigerian State, anything that is not in line with Patriotic Citizenship must be discouraged. This includes electoral violence which involves killing and destruction of properties belonging to people of different tribes. The government at different levels must frown at this and bring perpetrators to justice with adequate compensation on the affected victims. Thus, the effect of electoral violence on Patriotic Citizenship has been established.

Theoretical and Empirical Discourse

It is important to state here that sociological discourse on the theory of violent political behaviour is derived from electoral violence. It argues that such acts are centered on a number of theories such as frustration-aggression, aggressive cue, relative deprivation; rising expectation; systemic hypothesis; and group conflict theories. However, this study adopts the Aggressive cue theory because the theory emphasizes that acts of aggression are predisposed by the existence of socially learnt cues or environmental situations, which makes engaging in aggression acceptable. Politics in Africa creates serious and numerous electoral violence. This is not the case with developed and solid democracies that have adequate models within the framework of their political machineries. It is important to note that electoral violence promotes insecurity. This makes it uncertain for anyone to embark on a journey within the country without having to be sure what the threat along the highway could be. There have been situations where Nigerians living abroad travel into the country for a purpose and got killed before they travelled back to the foreign land where they sojourn. This insecurity challenges are more frequent during election seasons and are very daring.

The questions that come to mind are; is the blood of any Nigerian worth any political ambition? Must you govern over a people by force in a democracy? The thugs that are armed with live rounds and hard drugs, can they be sane again after the political attainment? Can Patriotic Citizenship be encouraged through vile means? Does ethnic hatred promote Patriotic Citizenship? These rhetorical only lends weight to the fact that electoral violence cannot promote unity to any state. Africa politics is blemished with so much insincerity and interest from the party in power. In the context of African political setting, political parties could be commonly regarded as a group of people with the interest of governance at all levels. The question is, do they sincerely have the interest of the common man that voted them into power? The answer is usually known after their tenure in office. However, Patriotic Citizenship seeks to establish that the leadership must drive the spirit of nationhood rather than a Nigerian derogatory project.

Chabal and Daloz are of the view that what marks the political domain of African continent is an active connivance between the political elites and the populace, the former, to grease the palm of the latter, irrespective of the security implications. Thus, the interpretation of politics in Africa is a mode of operation in which it is both judicious and legitimate to switch from one registered political party to another without an undue concern for the political contradictions which such behaviour might appear to encourage. Chabal and Caloz reiterated that an understanding that electoral victory may not always determine the legitimacy of the result, as determined by the Congo as well as the Cote D'Ivoire experience. It is for such reasons that Africa is said not to have gotten her democratic process right. The duo further added that the series of electoral victories in Nigeria's series of elections, already announced by various Electoral commissions in favour of certain candidates but later up-turned by the judiciary lends credence to the above assertion about Congo and Cote D' Ivoire respectively.

It is pertinent to note that the electoral violence that is witnessed today did not start in the Fourth Republic. Its root was during the colonial rule in Nigeria. Adelabu opines that the origin of political party conflict and electoral violence in Nigeria stemmed from the activities of political parties in vogue then. This can be understood but this study wonders why the colonialists did not do eradicate it. Although it is not surprising as the system of government of the colonial masters was, 'divide and rule.' Thus, the people have to be divided while you rule over them.

To Adelabu, Nigeria had no political party but a crowd. He emphasized that the distinguishing characteristics of a genuine political party should be in the generic words, ideas, ideal and ideology. This is very apt and could be said to have followed the various Republics. However, this study will not jump into assumptions. Do our political parties have what was portrayed of the parties in the First Republic? Adelabu further added that 'as a start, there must be an idea in the minds of the adherent, and when the idea permeates every aspect of the believer's life and it is internalised, it then becomes his particular system of thoughts as well as his ideology. It is when an ideology so dominates the life of individuals in a group and becomes the premier of faith and formal association into the think tank of a genuine political party.' This study agrees with this concept and is of the view that Patriotic Citizenship which would have long been in our daily routine had already been truncated before independence. In sincere terms the views of Adelabu is line with Chabal and Daloz's as the true reflection of Nigerian politics, "where the meaning of election and its purpose of having square pegs in square holes are glaringly absent. Since party affiliation is all about a forum to have access to the state's treasury for the comfort of the political contractor, and his or her cronies, good governance, which can guarantee both human and state security, is secondary."

These are empirical experiences of the First Republic. In another vein, Ige also contended that the prevalence of electoral violence is the product of the porous political structure in Nigeria. "He recalled his disappointment at the manner Zik was blocked through electoral manipulation and revealed that Zik never took his defeat in his bid to go to the Central Legislature like a sportsman, because Zik left Ibadan, rushed to the East, his region of birth, with psychological depression as a result of electoral manipulation. In his reflection, Ige is of the view that the electoral fraud visited in the nationalist may affect the electoral process in Nigeria in the near future."

These empirical experiences did not show that Nigeria had transformed in the way that she conducts her democratic process. Ibiam submits that:

> "Our first federal elections ended in a nightmare for all of us… We purposely and knowingly exalted dishonesty, while truth and decency were flogged and cowed to submission. In the recent Western Nigeria parliamentary election, our country became once again the cynosure of world eyes and a target for unwelcome global criticism. Surely, nobody can be happy about this our recent escapades in parliamentary democracy."

It is therefore, important to state here that the consistent dishonesty and lack of trust among the politicians led to enormous insecurity and uncontrollable political violent conflicts that have continued from one republic to another. The constant blaming of the military in politics was only hypocritical as the democratic actors only plunged the country into series of chaos and violent conflicts which have culminated into what is experienced in the Fourth Republic. Although this study is in full support of democratic governance, it expects the democrats to have Patriotic Citizenship in their minds as that come up with policies and programmes.

Strategic Approaches Towards Electoral Violence and Conflict Management in Nigeria

Elections in Africa have become one of the most important necessities since the end of colonialism. It is very engaging and a contentious feature of the political life across the continent. A few Africa's democracies are on the path of what Patriotic Citizenship and Service looks out for while many of them leave much to be desired as the people wallow continually in abject poverty. The outcomes of the more recent elections have been remarkably diverse, and the relationship between elections and conflict management is widely debated throughout the world. That of the countries in Africa have been badly rated in the peace management process.

Conflict Management therefore, involves established provisions and regulatory procedures for dealing with conflicts whenever they exist. In another vein, it can be said to be the interference in an ongoing conflict process in such a way as to contain, and if possible: reduce the level of violence and destruction; prevent the vertical escalation towards the use of weapons of mass destruction and prevent the horizontal expansion into other theaters. This is to avert unnecessary destruction of lives and properties. Importantly, elections can either help to reduce tensions by reconstituting legitimate government, or they can exacerbate them by further polarizing highly conflictual societies especially in Africa. This study examines the relationship between elections, especially electoral systems, and conflict management in Nigeria. It will help in defining different roles elections can play in democratization and conflict management.

This study has proffered certain strategic approaches towards electoral violence and conflict management in the Nigerian State. There are four main scientific and research methods for handling the typical Nigeria's types of conflicts. These are, avoidance, confrontation, third party decision making and the joint problem solving. However, it is important to state here that the first two methods will be appropriate for the Nigerian State due to the complexity of the conflicts. Suffice to state here that empirical knowledge from various scholars in research methodology, the efficacy of the third decision making and joint problem solving which were not properly exploited in the past culminated in the serious electoral challenges that we witness today in Nigeria. Although the challenge of June 12 has been well addressed by the President Muhammadu Buhari's government, through the last two approaches mentioned here, the killing of the Ogoni 9 still pervades and makes the environmental conflict very difficult to be forgotten. The banishment of some traditional rulers across the country who were not sympathetic to certain ruling parties has created more electoral violence than peace. These are issues that are very difficult to solve except by exploring the problem solving mechanism. Thus, the theory of conflict dynamics states that:

> "All conflicts go through a preliminary dispute phase and may also go through one or more hostilities and post-hostilities phase. In each phase, identifiable factors generate pressures that may influence the cause of the case toward the next threshold and transition into another phase. These factors may be offset by other influential factors that tend towards the prevention of that transition."

The 2023 election was the country's largest-ever, most youthful electorate with new technologies and fully deployed military assets across the country. This means that the challenges of the election as it came out to be will be very violent and will have the variables that are not credible. This study will not go into details on the flaws of the electoral process but will simple ask if the actors in their various activities proved that they support the term Patriotic Citizenships for the Nigerian State. The hypothesis earlier adduced in this study states that conflicts have phases which are both hostilities and post –hostilities stages. It is important to note that in each stage there are distinguishable factors that could bring about pressures which would influence the course of the conflict however complex. This is either to obstruct efforts at maximizing or to advance the course of dowsing tension. Significantly, the changes could make or mar efforts at transforming the conflict stage. It is for this reason that policy decisions should be geared towards violence minimixing factors. This will enable a win-win situation, thus prevent a conflict situation. In the case of the 2015 presidential election between the incumbent President Goodluck Ebele Jonathan of the People Democratic Party and President Muhammadu Buhari, of the All People Congress, the intervention of various members of the Nigerian society as well as the international community and Presidents of countries like President Barak Obama of the United States of America, encouraged President Jonathan to concede power which many presidents will not accept. He simply stated:

"My ambition is not worth the blood of any Nigerian."

In another vein, the emergence of the Boko Haram Sect is another aspect that had to do with an aspect of management of conflicts. It is a passing phase which can be handled using the multiplication of conflict management mechanisms. Thus, the cooperation of neighbouring countries in building a strong multinational force as well as other methods like granting amnesty to repentant Nigerian Boko Haram members, has gone a long way to help solve some aspects of the conflict. A very important giant stride that this study will like to commend is the peace building institution which is in place. It is the Peace and Conflict Commission in the Federal Capital Territory, Abuja. The commission has since set into motion machineries towards combating various conflict situations thereby averting major conflicts such as electoral violence from escalating.

The Nigerian electoral violence challenges have been issues that have pestered the country for many decades. This has made it look like a normal problem and a way of life creating so much suspicion and distrust. These are challenges with multiplicity of strands.

Analysis of Provisions and Legal Measures Against Electoral Violence/Electoral Offences

This study is interested in the provision made against electoral violence and offences. There are quite enough provisions of the criminal and civil law which should be able to curb electoral violence as well as its offences. The foundation of electoral violence in Nigeria which started before independence has been attributed to social and political marginalization, poverty, unemployment and under-employment and other unbearable human problems which are built on intervening processes that connect to electoral violence which has direct relationship with arms proliferation. Nigerian electoral act 2006 precisely has several provisions targeted against electoral violence. Importantly, Section 97(5) of the acts provides that no political party or member of a political party shall retain, organize, train or equip any person or group of persons for the purpose of enabling them to be employed for use or display of physical force or coercion in promoting any political objective or interest in such a manner as to arouse reasonable apprehension that they are organized, trained or equipped for that purpose. This is a very good one.

Also, Section 97 (6), no political party candidate or any person shall keep or use private security organization, vanguard or any other group or individual by whatever name for the purpose of providing security, assisting or aiding the political party or candidate in whatever manner during campaigns, rallies, processions or elections. The punishments prescribed for contravention of the above subsections in the case of an individual is a fine of 500,000 or imprisonment for a term of six months.

Additionally, Section 98 of the act states that no candidate, person or group of persons shall directly or indirectly threaten anybody with the use of force or violence during any political campaign in order to compel that person or any other person to support a political party or candidate. Breach of this provision will attract a fine of N50,000 or imprisonment for a term of six months in the case of an individual or a fine N250,000 in the first instance and N500,000 for subsequent offence in the case of a political party. There are other aspects of the electoral act that prohibits and states offence for certain electoral crimes.

However, some observers have expressed their take on the electoral act as it affects the various election violations.

"Many of this violence have been a public display of egregious partisan violence; so we ask why this is occurring. The stakes are high and politicians are engaged in gruesome politics but the incentives are not there to deter such violence," Mr Stocker said. This was further amplified by another observer:

> "While the 2022 electoral act proscribes penalties for offences, enforcement of such penalties is lacking. It is therefore the responsibility of all stakeholders invested in this election to change the incentives around electoral violence and to hold their people accountable for their actions."

During the conference organized by Kimpact Development Initiative (KDI) in 2023, several observations were made by dignitaries that attended it. The topic for discussion was titled; "timely and germane as we speedily count down to the 2023 elections."

In his submission, Basil Idegwu, the representative of the Inspector General of Police said the police have been making adequate preparations to ensure that electoral violence is put in check or mitigated ahead of the elections. He reiterated that:

> "We started by carrying out our threat analysis all over the federation and we will continue to update these threats as this will help in the deployment of our

personnel and resources," he said. The representative of the Inspector General further added that:

"We are also working closely with other security agencies to ensure that we carry out the well-harmonised deployment of personnel. We are equally working with our intelligence assets to make sure that perpetrators of this violence are put in check or arrested," Mr Idegwu concluded.

The Commandant General of the Civil Defence Corps, Mr Ahmed Audi commended Kimpact Development Initiative (KDI) for hosting the programme. He reiterated that:

"We as a people unfortunately are yet to get our electoral processes right but it is hoped that this first high-level national dialogue will painstakingly and decisively be laid to rest all the triggers and problems that have impaired our electoral system. Consequently, debasing and retarding our essence into the world of civilised nations," the Nigeria Security and Civil Defence Corps Boss said. He further re-emphasized that:

"We therefore must come together to salvage our electoral system," Mr Audi said. "The forthcoming 2023 election is very critical and of utmost importance to the survival and growth of our democracy. And so all hands must be on deck to ensure that the election is credible, free and fair."

Unfortunately, Nigeria recorded 339 incidents of election violence in 2022. This data was collated by the Kimpact Development Initiative. This is very high and not encouraging for Patriotic Citizenship in Nigeria. It certainly cannot offer excellent service.

Conclusion

The electoral process in Nigeria has seriously affected the Patriotic Citizenship zeal with a surge in violent conflicts during electoral seasons. These are the persistence in attaining selfish interests as against that of the wellbeing of the common man. It is a fertile recruitment season of all sorts of persons who might not have the value for true Patriotic Citizenship. During the elections season, Nigerians are further divided in the eyes of foreigners that are not particularly interested in the progress of the nation. With the rich resources of the Nigerian State, this study abhors that her people should suffer in abject poverty. Rather, her citizens should embrace true Patriotic Citizenship at all level irrespective of the tribe and tongue that may differ. Unfortunately, during election seasons, partisan violence escalates along ethnic and sectarian lines. This produces a spillover effect resulting in multiple rounds of revenge killings across the nation. This affects unity and Patriotic Citizenship.

References

Adeyinka O. Banwo (2003:11) "Political Violence and Democratisation in Nigeria" in B. Olasupo Electoral Violence in Nigeria, Lagos, Frankad Publishers.

Armed Conflict Location and Event Data (ACLED) by C Raleigh, 2010. Cited by 1902.

Afolabi Ayeni-Akeke (2003:69) "Electoral Violence and the Democratisation Project: "The Nigerian Experience" in B. Olasupo Electoral Violence in Nigeria.

American Scientific Research Journal for Engineering, Technology, and Sciences (ASRJETS) (2019) Volume 54, No 1, pp 173-184175

Albert, Marco and Adetula emphasising the adversial level of electoral violence in Perspectives on the 2003 Elections in Nigeria.

Bola Ige (1995:76) People, Politics and Politicians of Nigeria, Ibadan, Heineman Educational Books Plc.

Chabal and Daloz (1999) Africa Works: Disorder as political Instrument. Publisher; James Currey Publishers 1999.

G. Hyden and M. Bratton (1992) Government and Polities in Africa, Boulder, Renner Publishers.

Kimpact Development Initiative, 2022.

Osisioma B.C. Nwolise (2007) Electoral violence and Nigeria's 2007 elections. Published Online:1 Oct 2007https://hdl.handle.net/10520/EJC32440Cited by:2

SAGE, Corwin Press, Paul Chapman Publishing, Pine Forge Press, SAGE Reference, SAGE Science and Scolari (US and Europe websites) imprints.

Chapter

10

Human Resource Management and Post-Traumatic Disorder: An effect on Patriotic Citizenship

Introduction

Human Resource Management (HRM) has played a very significant role in the success or failure of many organisations across the globe. The quality of workers that you find in an organisation will to a great extent determine the output and financial growth that it should expect. If an organisation decides to employ half-baked professionals and mediocre, such a firm is likely to have taunted growth and the efficiency that is expected. This also applies to establishments that do not have the Human Resource Management department distinct or expressed as it is done in corporate organisations.

International firms such as the coca cola in particular have stood out in quality and excellence due to the outstanding strides of over a century. The essence of the Human Resource Management is to help in the understanding of the complex and changing context of Human Resource Management and the importance of resilience and sustainability in turbulent business locations.

Human Resource Management therefore, is the strategic and coherent approach to the effective and efficient management of people in a company or organization. This holistically helps their business to gain a competitive advantage. It is designed to maximize employee performance in service of an employer's strategic objectives. If the objectives are not achieved, the Human Resource Management has failed in its duties. Rather, the Human Resource Management should be proactive as well as create awareness of contemporary Human Resource Manangement issues in readiness for being future human resource developments challenges. This will go long way to curb lots of problems for the organisations. This is the same with a country. If the wrong people are brought to power in what is known as KAKISTOCRACY that country's citizens will suffer so much. They will probably yearn for a change like what was witnessed during the Arab Spring which started in 17th December 2010. The goals were; Democracy Economic freedom; Employment, Free elections; Human rights; Reforms; Regime change.

It is important to briefly look at the history of Human Resource Management. Various attempts have been made towards tracing the historical development of HRM. They are concentrated to specific period of time and experiences of certain countries such as the USA, the UK and Asia (Nambervis et al, 2011; Kelly 2003; Ogier, 2003). Africa only took a leaf from these countries later in the 21st century. The evolution of the Human Resource Management can be traced right from the prehistoric times through to the post-modern world. While Africa could be said to have had the Human Resource Management strategies. However, it was not practiced the way it is today.

This study wishes to look at the definition of Human Resource Management. According to Armstrong (2006), Human Resource Management (HRM) a strategic and coherent approach to the management of an organisation's most valued assets - the people working there who individually and collectively contribute to the achievement of its objectives. It is significant to add here that

Human Resource Management or Human Resource is a function in organisations designed to maximise employee's performance in service of their employer's strategic objectives, (Johnson, 2009). HR is primarily concerned with how people are managed within organisations, focusing on policies and systems. Therefore, Human Resource departments and units in organisations are responsible for a number of activities, including employee recruitment, training and development, performance appraisal and rewards (managing pay and benefit systems) (Poawe and Boon, 2009). Human Resource is also concerned with Industrial relations, that is balancing of organisational practices with regulations arising from collective bargaining and governmental laws (Klerck,2009).

In an attempt to re-evaluate human resource management, this study takes a critical look at the problematic status of post traumatic disorder. This will go a long way to assist proffer solutions to this problem. This disorder cuts across workers in different categories, industries with heavy machines, hospitals, the military, security agencies etc. It is also known as Post –Traumatic Stress Disorder.

Post –Traumatic Stress Disorder is a mental health condition that's triggered by a terrifying event either by experiencing it or witnessing it. Symptoms may include flashbacks, nightmares and severe anxiety, as well as uncontrollable thoughts about the event. It is important to note that most people who go through traumatic events may have temporary difficulty adjusting and coping, but with time and good self-care, they usually get better. If the symptoms get worse, last for months or even years, and interfere with your day-to-day functioning, you may have Post –Traumatic Stress Disorder. For example, soldiers with terminal injuries or health caused by violent conflicts, insurgency or war challenges may find it difficult to cope within their families' environments. Many of these officers and men are accommodated within military hospitals where they are taken care of. It is necessary to state here that getting effective treatment after Post –Traumatic

Stress Disorder symptoms develop can be critical to reduce symptoms and improve the condition of the person involved.

The traumatic effect of Post –Traumatic Stress Disorder cannot be underestimated. The person that is affected who was probably a healthy and sport like person is probably disabled and cannot hold any employment. Post –Traumatic Stress Disorder also destroys the family structure as it reduces the self-confidence and social status of a person. It causes lack of funds for basic household maintenance as well as for other essentials, including school fees. The result of all these are constant friction and feuds in the family, usually with one spouse demanding money to pay for housekeeping.

The Purpose of this paper is to discuss Human Resource Management and its Post Traumatic Disorder. The paper will cover: Conceptual Clarifications, Overview of Human Resource Management and Post Traumatic Disorder. Furthermore, it will discuss the Effects of Post Traumatic Disorder. Finally, it will proffer solutions to Post Traumatic Disorder Challenges. The study does not have a specific period that it covers. This is because Post Traumatic Disorder has been with man right from the pre medieval days.

Conceptual Clarifications

There are two variables in this study, which are: Human Resource Management and Post Traumatic Disorder. These would be conceptualised and the relationship between them established.

Human Resource Management

Human resource management (HRM) is the process of employing people, training them, compensating them, developing policies relating to them, and developing strategies to retain them. As a field, Human Resource Management has undergone many changes over the last twenty years, giving it an even more important role in today's organizations. However, in Alo's (19999: 157), the study of human resource management practices in Nigeria completely portray different situations depicted. However, the definition earlier put forward is very apt and can be considered for this paper.

Post Traumatic Disorder

This is a condition where people with terrible life experiences such as war, death, disaster become paranoid. Post –Traumatic Stress Disorder is a mental health condition that's triggered by a terrifying event — either experiencing it or witnessing it. Post-traumatic stress disorder symptoms may start within one month of a traumatic event, but sometimes symptoms may not appear until years after the event. These symptoms cause significant problems in social or work situations and in relationships. They can also interfere with one's ability to go about your normal daily tasks. It is important to state here that several injustices especially in professional job posts could be responsible for a particular aspect of Post –Traumatic Stress Disorder. It is therefore necessary for a there to be a fair and equity place where people carry out their task without fear or favour.

Post –Traumatic Stress Disorder symptoms can be distinguished into 4 groups or types: These are the; intrusive memories, avoidance, negative changes in thinking and mood, and changes in physical and emotional reactions. It is also important to note that its symptoms can vary over time or vary from person to person. The same type of variable might affect a different victim in a different way. In the present day society, much have been seen of successful young people who commit suicide either by hanging, falling off the cliff or jump into the lagoon. In the military too, there have been a few incidences where a soldier shot sporadically and killed his colleagues. These cases could be observed and handled properly at an early stage.

Relationship Between Human Resource Management and Post Traumatic Disorder

Human Resource Management in Nigeria, has developed very fast with lots of reforms especially with the upsurge in the output from tertiary education and the inelastic labour absorptive capacity of the Nigerian labour market for the services of university and polytechnic graduates. Although both the government and private sector have done so much in trying open up more job opportunities, the population of qualified professionals seems to be on the rise. Due to the global economic decline and high cost of production, most organizations' try to downsize to accommodate their capital expenditure.

On the contrary, most of the organizations seem to have problems due to inadequate shelter good health care system and other benefits for its workers. Many too are unable to cater for the ones that are retired or laid off. All these lead to Post –Traumatic Stress Disorder. It's normal to experience upsetting and confusing thoughts when confronted with serious life challenges. However, these could lead to Post –Traumatic Stress Disorder depending on the traumatic challenges that one faces after leaving the job. Some pension service providers do not have the requisite standard to offer such services. This creates a lot of problem to the pensioners sometimes leading to Post –Traumatic Stress Disorder. On the contrary, if the organization is able to manage the affairs of its retiree properly, in the aspect of welfare, good health system and proper payment of pension, the challenges of Post –Traumatic Stress Disorder will be highly reduced. There is therefore, a direct relationship between Human Resource Management and Post –Traumatic Stress Disorder.

Overview of Human Resource Management and Post Traumatic Disorder

Having looked at the variable earlier discussed, this study intends to holistically have some details about Post –Traumatic Stress Disorder.

Post –Traumatic Stress Disorder is the Psychological reaction occurring after a highly stressful event and typically characterized by flashbacks, recurrent nightmares, and avoidance of reminders of the event; depression and anxiety are often present. It is significant to state here that traumatic events that can lead to Post –Traumatic Stress Disorder include automobile accidents, rape or assault, military combat, torture, and such natural disasters as floods, fires, or earthquakes. Long-term effects can include marital and family problems, difficulties at work, and abuse of alcohol and other drugs. Antidepressant medication and psychotherapy, including group therapy, are used in treating the disorder. However, this depends on the extent of the challenge on the victim. Post –Traumatic Stress Disorder can be further classified into the various categories as stated below:

Intrusive memories: Symptoms of intrusive memories may include:

a. Recurrent, unwanted distressing memories of the traumatic event
b. Reliving the traumatic event as if it were happening again (flashbacks)
c. Upsetting dreams or nightmares about the traumatic event
d. Severe emotional distress or physical reactions.

Avoidance . Symptoms of avoidance may include; Trying to avoid thinking or talking about the traumatic event and avoiding places, activities or people that remind you of the traumatic event.

Negative changes in thinking and mood. Symptoms of negative changes in thinking and mood may include:

(i) Negative thoughts about yourself, other people or the world
(ii) Hopelessness about the future
(iii) Memory problems
(iv) Difficulty in maintaining close relationships
(v) Feeling detached from family and friends

(vi) Lack of interest in activities
(viii) Difficulty in experiencing positive emotions you once enjoyed
(ix) Feeling emotionally numb

Changes in physical and emotional reactions. Symptoms of changes in physical and emotional reactions (also called arousal symptoms) may result to being easily startled or frightened. In some intense cases, the victim always be on guard. These are peculiar to emotional trauma caused by incidents such as experience, armed robbery attacks, kidnapping or even rape. In some other instances victims could engage in heavy drinking habit which makes them very erratic. In another instance, victims could be overwhelmed with guilt and shame.

Intensity of symptoms: This study wishes to reiterate that Post –Traumatic Stress Disorder symptoms can vary in intensity over time. One may have more Post –Traumatic Stress Disorder symptoms when exposed to stressed in general, or when one come across reminders of what happened in the past. There are certain traumatic experiences that one will not wish to happen to anyone. For example, a man who lost his two legs in battle will always feel bad when he hears any form of violent conflict such as wars. Or a lady that was gang raped will hate the sight of men in a group.

The Effect of Post Traumatic Disorder

Post –Traumatic Stress Disorder has several devastating effect on the organisation where the victim worked and the society as a whole. It is worse with the military especially with epileptic payments of monthly pension and allowances to those injured and sick. Someone with Post –Traumatic Stress Disorder often recalls the traumatic event through nightmares and flashbacks, and may experience feelings of isolation, irritability and guilt. They may also have problems sleeping, such as insomnia, and find concentrating difficult. There are other characteristics that are associated with Post –Traumatic Stress Disorder such as depression.

Depression is categorised by feelings of sadness or low mood lasting more than a few days. Depression and Post –Traumatic Stress Disorder commonly occur together. Almost one in 10 adults suffer from depression in a given year in Africa and Nigeria in particular. This is due to the high rate and poverty and the poor health system. Additionally, the poor state of veterans' welfare and their sustenance is very deplorable. Depression can affect your ability to perform daily functions and can diminish your quality of life. It also has adverse effects on eating and sleeping habits. Depression is three to five times more likely to be diagnosed in people who are living with Post –Traumatic Stress Disorder. Other important effects of Post –Traumatic Stress Disorder are as discussed below:

Effect on Families. People suffering from Post –Traumatic Stress Disorder are likely to have a lot of financial challenges which most often leads to several other problems such as divorce, inability to take care of the family, frustration and many others. This is particularly common with the military where such problems are more obvious than other professions. It is important to state here that shortly after there is such a challenge as Post –Traumatic Stress Disorder in a military family, the victim is likely to be rejected after a short time due to the fact that wealth is not gathered in the military. It is even difficult to sustain a home after service not to talk about the ex-military personnel with Post –Traumatic Stress Disorder. This is case in many countries in Africa.

In some parts too, the challenges of people living with disability are much. They are discriminated by their family members and looked upon like outcasts who have incurred the wrath of the local gods of their lands. Veterans have always had it very tough during the regimes of the Fourth Republic until President Muhammadu Buhari's government that made effort to tackle some of the problems associated with the Nigerian Military Veterans. Even the main issues such as the Debarment Allowance which has to do with the restrain from using military skills by veterans against the state have not been properly addressed even with the many promises. This is very discouraging and against the Patriotic Citizenship strides that the Veterans have put in the service of their nation.

Other places of interest are the disabled educated and skillful Nigerians with Post –Traumatic Stress Disorder. They are discriminated in workplaces and areas where most of them excel. Unfortunately, due to their vulnerabilities they are prone to abuses of all sort which sometimes leads to their total inabilities to survive.

Effect on Organisations. The essence of life in a workplace is for families to be taken care of by the bread winner. Either a man or woman is part of the success of a thriving organisation to which they could be in some ways custodians of their families. Each profession has its challenges which can also be categorized into low risk, medium and high risk jobs. The rate at which Post –Traumatic Stress Disorder is experienced also differs from one profession to another. It is also important to note that Post –Traumatic Stress Disorder can affect the least expected in the society. For example, what will make a medical doctor to jump into a Lagoon in Lagos? There are other suicide cases that can hardly be placed in terms of the class in the society the victims are and their success stories.

Post –Traumatic Stress Disorder is very pronounced in the military especially among the veterans. Long before now, the veterans were not properly managed. Their pensions were given to some service providers who made a mess of the whole post service little entitlement of men and women who served their country meritoriously. Many of them lost their children and wives to abject poverty and drugs. It was very difficult to make ends meet as a lot of them died of Post –Traumatic Stress Disorder. The society that they found themselves was not disciplined which made the problem worse. However, the government of President Mohammadu Buhari has done a lot to alleviate the sufferings of the veterans. There is however, the need to sustain this by successive regimes.

Suffice to state here that for the active military personnel, more concern has been shown on welfare with much focus on the relationship between combat and emotional health of military personnel. There is the need for this to be sustained.

Effect on the society: A society that is said to have many people suffering from Post –Traumatic Stress Disorder is not likely to be a sane one especially if most of these problems are drug related. In many areas, there are people living with disabilities who encounter very traumatic criminal threats especially the women among them. Everyday, these people witness terrible crimes where they reside. In slums and places that have little or no security presence, it is worse. Some events that cause trauma can either be rape, accidents, illnesses, violent assaults, and many more. Where the government is able to carry out a background check on those living with Post –Traumatic Stress Disorder, it is easier to proffer solution to this problem. There is therefore the need for proper profiling of places where people reside in high numbers so as to curb some criminal activities that could be in disguise for Post –Traumatic Stress Disorder.

Solutions to Post Traumatic Disorder

Post –Traumatic Stress Disorder can be successfully treated, even when it develops many years after a traumatic event. However, this must be closely observed so that it does not generate to something worse. Treatment depends on the severity of symptoms and how soon they occur after the traumatic event. It is important to state here that certain behavioural traits that seem unethical should be closely observed especially if such a person bears arms. The following treatment will suffice:

   a. watchful waiting – monitoring the symptoms to see whether they improve or get worse without treatment
   b. The use of antidepressants – such as paroxetine or sertraline
   c. Use of therapies, such as trauma-focused.

However, if the symptom persists and the condition gets worse, there is the need to see a doctor or a mental health professional. This will go a long way to solve the problem. Getting treatment as soon as possible can help prevent Post –Traumatic Stress Disorder symptoms from getting worse.

Conclusion

Human Resource Management has been with mankind throughout history. However, the field became more prominent in the early part of the 20th century. Today, it has taken the centre stage of many organizations. Most work places employ professionals that will build capacity for their organizations. However, these organizations usually have challenges associated with the people in their work force either while in active service or after they retire either voluntarily or due to a health challenge known as Post –Traumatic Stress Disorder. There is therefore the need for organisations or government to take care of their personnel either serving or retired with the challenge of Post –Traumatic Stress Disorder.

It is important to state here that Post –Traumatic Stress Disorder has a number of causes that include psychological trauma, which can be caused by emotional or physical abuse. These traumas could be wars or violent conflicts, accident, rape, war, natural disaster, illness, violent attack and others. People who are suffering from Post –Traumatic Stress Disorder have different symptoms that can last for a couple of days but lift with time (Friedman, 2000). Some people have nightmares, feel numb, and sometimes experience difficulties in trying to forget what happened. To some people, the symptoms are triggered by activities that make them remember what took place. This could be very traumatic. For example, a young electrician assigned to repair a damaged electric wire on a pole fell and eventually had his two hands amputated. This will be difficult to ever forget. There is therefore the need for such cases to be rehabilitated by the organization or government with constant free treatment.

Some of the types of treatment offered to Post –Traumatic Stress Disorder include cognitive and behavioral therapy (Myers, 2007). This is where the therapist encourages the victim to carefully expose oneself to feelings, thoughts, and even situations that will help one remember the trauma. During this treatment, one thinks about the upsetting things and then replaces them with thoughts that have a better picture. For example, if the trauma was caused by an event of war, one exposes him or herself to things that are related to that event. In this case, one can watch a movie about war so that he or she can remember the event. He or she can also think about raising a fight against someone else and then replace the thought with a peaceful moment. There is therefore the need for those with Post –Traumatic Stress Disorder to be early diagnosed and treated.

Reccommendation

It is recommended that:

a. Organisations should take care of their personnel either serving or retired with the challenge of Post –Traumatic Stress Disorder.
b. People with Post –Traumatic Stress Disorder of terrible conditions with the loss of any part of the body should be rehabilitated by the government with constant free treatment.
c. Those with Post –Traumatic Stress Disorder should be early diagnosed and treated.

References

American Psychiatric Association. (2022). Trauma- and Stressor-Related Disorders. In <u>Diagnostic and Statistical Manual of Mental Disorders</u> (5th ed., text rev.).

Bichitra Nanda Patra and Siddharth Sarkar. Adjustment Disorder: Current Diagnostic Status. Indian J Psychol Med. 2013 Jan-Mar; 35(1): 4–9

Bremner JD, Southwick SM, Johnson DR, Yehuda R, Charney DS, Childhood physical abuse and combat-related posttraumatic stress disorder in Vietnam veterans. The American journal of psychiatry. 1993 Feb; [PubMed PMID: 8422073]

Bryant RA, Friedman MJ, Spiegel D, Ursano R, Strain J, A review of acute stress disorder in DSM-5. Depression and anxiety. 2011 Sep; [PubMed PMID: 21910186]

Charuvastra A, Cloitre M, Social bonds and posttraumatic stress disorder. Annual review of psychology. 2008; [PubMed PMID: 17883334] Current Diagnostic Status. *Indian J Psychol Med*. 2013 Jan-Mar; 35(1): 4–9.

Friedman, M (2000). Post-Traumatic Stress Disorder: Journal of the Treatment Strategies, 32(6), 47.

G Kelly, 2003, The Psychology of personal constructs: Volume two: clinical diagnosis and psychotherapy

Harvard Medical School. (2007). National Comorbidity Survey (NCS). (2017, August 21). Data Table 2: 12-month prevalence DSM-

Kinchin, D. (2004). Research advances in rheumatoid arthritis. Journal of the American Medical Association, 285(5), 648-650 M Armstrong, S Taylor 2006 Human Resource Strategies and the retention of older RNs

Ogier, 2003 History, Evolution and Development of Human Resource

M Armstrong, S Taylor 2006 Human Resource Strategies and the retention of older RNs Sherin JE, Nemeroff CB, Post-traumatic stress disorder: the neurobiological impact of psychological trauma. Dialogues in clinical neuroscience. 2011; [PubMed PMID: 22034143]

Sherin JE, Nemeroff CB, Post-traumatic stress disorder: the neurobiological impact of psychological trauma. Dialogues in clinical neuroscience. 2011; [PubMed PMID: 22034143]

Wang Z, Zhu H, Yuan M, Li Y Qiu C, Ren Z, Yuan C, Lui S, Gong Q, Zhang W, The resting-state functional connectivity of amygdala subregions associated with post-traumatic stress symptom and sleep quality in trauma survivors. European archives of psychiatry and clinical neuroscience. 2020 Feb 12; [PubMed PMID: 32052123]

Yehuda R, Hoge CW, McFarlane AC, Vermetten E, Lanius RA, Nievergelt CM, Hobfoll SE, Koenen KC, Neylan TC, Hyman SE, Post-traumatic stress disorder. Nature reviews. Disease primers. 2015 Oct 8; [PubMed PMID: 27189040]

Chapter

11

The Nigerian Military as Protectors of Democratic Stability and Patriotic Citizenship

Introduction

Developed democracies across the world have the military as their vital institution that helps to protect their democratic governments. Although they mostly at the background in the affairs of their nations, that of Africa are at the forefront due to the security challenges that their countries face in different dimensions. Nigerian Armed Forces or the Nigerian Military is the number one democrat in the Fourth Republic. It's role right from the beginning of the republic has been that of total allegiance to its constitutional duties. The military has the interest of the nation at all times and has steadily and successfully worked with successive democratic governments since the inception of the Fourth Republic in 1999. This study sees the military as that cohesive force with a bond of unity helping to ensure that the Nigerian State does not have any form of crack. It is important to note that this study does not see the military as an alternative to democratic governance but an example of what the study seeks in terms of Patriotic Citizenship and Service. Although there have been many studies about the military incursion into power, such studies failed to state the conditions of extreme hardship that the common man is put into and the spate of insecurity in the countries. In most cases, it is the political elites that lure the military to intervene to avoid total anarchy.

It is important to state the Role of the Military in a Democracy as practiced across the globe. It is an ever-relevant concern which was already raised by Plato 2500 years. The principle of political control of the armed forces as we know it today is rooted in the concept of a representative democracy. It refers to the supremacy of civilian institutions, based on popular sovereignty, over the defense and security policy-making apparatus, including the military leadership. This study challenges the prevailing and long believe by some schools of thought about the orthodoxy in constitutional theory that a constitutional role for the military in an emerging democracy necessarily hinders democratic progress. The Nigerian military have played, a democracy-promoting role in the initial phases of a transition from autocracy to constitutional democracy.

The conventional theory which assumes that all militaries are hegemonic and praetorian institutions that must be completely disconnected from the civilian realm is not accepted by this study. This conception is erroneous considering the very significant role that the military played in the Fourth Republic especially with the coming on stage of the Boko Haram Sect that was determined to sack the Nigerian democracy. Theorizing the democracy-promoting has a long way to do with analyzing the democracy as well as promoting the constitutional role that the Nigerian military has been embarked in. This study is of the view that the military should be commended and be part of the engaging society rather be placed far into the distance as recommended by some orthodox schools of thought.

Conceptual Discourse about the military as Protectors of Democratic Stability and Patriotic Citizenship

This study started by discussing the conceptual variables and key issues such as Patriotic Citizenship. However, let us note that Citizenship has both objective and subjective meanings. The objective meaning sees citizens as those belonging to a political system by accident of birth, marriage, naturalization and nationalization. The subjective dimension locates the concept at the level of rights and obligations of an individual within the political system of a true democratic state. Additionally, Citizenship is conceived in a symbolic aspect which could be between the state and individual. This is defined as a regime of rights, privileges and duties (Adejumobi, 2005). Importantly, rights that belong to citizens are generally categorized into three aspects. These are civil, political and social (Marshall, 1964). Civil rights consist of the right to life, freedom of speech, thought, conscience, religion, liberty, fair hearing and the dignity of the human person. Political rights have to do with the taking part in the affairs of the state which includes the right to vote and be voted for in an election. Then social rights are the right to economic welfare, social security, the right to education and to live the life of a civilized being (Marshall,1964). However, it is important to note that these right are not the same in certain climes where the system of government is not democratic like the Republic of North Korea.

The Highly Educated Elite in the Fourth Republic

No nation in the world does not take advantage in her human resources especially when it to do important policies, deliberations on matters that affects the common man as well as crucial delicate decisions. These think tanks are the highly educated professionals who have distinguished themselves in different fields of studies.

Nigeria's highly educated elite may be traced deep into the colonial period itself (Colerman 1958; Ayandele 1974) They were part of those that fought for the country's independence. Many of them had their early education in Europe, the United Kingdom and the United States of America. The idea for true independence was very strong within them as they did their best to foster the various movements and agitations that led to the independence of Nigeria. They were the political class. Another group that were less visible was the second elite group, the "senior service" elite which took over the colonial administrative state through the 1950s and the first years after independence. They may be designated as the administrative, or bureaucratic, or "structural" (Post and Vickers 1973) elite. These two elite groups were closely bound together (Coleman 1958; Post and Vickers 1973, 43; Paden 1986, 230-45). However, by the early 1960s, a sharper separation was apparent between the political elite and the administrative elite (Post and Vickers 1973, 44). Up to the period of the first and second republic the political elite had deeply rooted themselves into the Nigerian political landscape criticizing any upset in the change in any government caused by their own errors. However, things began to take a different turn as majority of graduates and professionals emerged from the new institutions of higher education. They went into administrative roles within the public sector institutions.

Both groups of elites criticized the military for venturing into power blaming the latter for the woes of the country yet quite a number of the Presidents were former military leaders. While the policies and the constitutional reforms that were carried during the military regimes were actually done by selected outstanding academic elites, it is apparent then that the military in its Patriotic Citizenship drive had the interest of the nation at heart by not allowing any group of elite plunge her into yet another civil strife. Years after military incursion into power, the common man can readily tell the difference. This study is very particular about the way we hold our country and the ethnic divide that has continued to widen. It craves for Patriotic Citizenship at all levels. According to the Late Sonny Okosun of blessed memory:

"Let us help Nigeria, so that Nigeria will not die."

Other roles of the Military that Enhance Patriotic Citizenship

Apart from its constitutional primary roles, the military plays very significant role to enhance Patriotic Citizenship. The theoretical considerations to the reality on the ground is putting the country first in all that we do. The constitution anticipates in summary the following roles for the Armed Forces:

- Defend Nigeria's the territorial sovereignty of the state and participate in the collective defense in ECOWAS.
- Provide humanitarian aid
- Perform search and rescue missions
- Provide assistance in disasters
- Provide assistance in accidents
- Participate in maintaining public order, with and without arms, by
- Providing administrative assistance
- Performing protective functions
- Assisting the police in emergencies

This study reiterates that the military is the ultima ratio when police and border guard forces are not able to handle violent conflicts during very difficult and complex situations. The Nigerian Constitution openly prohibits any action, which could disturb the peaceful togetherness of the country or that which supports the preparation of any aggression.

The Theory of Civil- Military Relations

This study is of the view that civil-military relations theory applied to mature democratic states as well as the struggling ones. However, it is stronger in developed countries democracies. It emphasises that the important theoretical problem is how to maintain a military that sustains and protects democratic values, showing how the classic and still influential theories of Huntington and Janowitz were rooted respectively, in liberal and civic republican theories of democracy. This did not adequately solve this problem.

However, this study uses the situations on the ground to establish the relations between the military and the political elites, the relations of civilians to the military and the state as well as the multinational use of force. It further established a new theory of civil-military relations. One of them is on the premise that accounts for the circumstances that mature democracies presently face and tells how militaries can be sustained as they protect democratic values. Thus, it cannot be derived from either liberal or civic republican models of democracy, as Huntington and Janowitz tried to do, but might be derived from federalist models. This solves the challenge earlier posed. A cordial relation with the civil populace as well as political office holders will promote democracy and Patriotic Citizenship.

Suffice to state here that what is applicable in the Nigerian context is different from some states. For instance, while the Commander in Chief of the Nigerian Armed Forces is the President of the country, for the German Armed Forces it is not the Federal President but a civilian Minister of Defence who is in charge of both civilian and military officials. Thus, the constitution firmly secured the Primacy of Politics in the constitution and classified the Armed Forces as belonging to the system of constitutional organs without any concession. It is important to state here that the Minister of Defence is bound by the Federal Chancellor's authority of Germany to determine general policy guidelines as it affects the military and its operations.

Conclusion

The role of the military since the beginning of the Fourth Republic has been very commendable. So much have been achieved in terms of helping to stabilize the Nigerian democracy which has been experiencing so much challenges. The military has also shown itself very strong in propagating the oneness which Patriotic Citizenship demonstrates. However, there has been so many political rascalism and deceitful hypocrisy which this study is against. This study believes that ethnic militias should not be idolized in the face of a functional and successful military. It unequivocally demands that the Fourth Republic should unite Nigeria against all odds. All regions especially the three major tribes should produce Presidents of the country in the Fourth Republic. This will encourage Patriotic Citizenship.

References

Acemoglu, D., Ticchi, D. and Vindigni, A. 2010. A Theory of Military Dictatorships. American Economic Journal: Macroeconomics, 2(1): 1-42

Badie, B., Berg-Schlosser, D. and Morlino, L. 2011. Military Rule. International Encyclopedia of Political Science, 8.

Ball, A.R. and Guy-Peters, B. 2000. Modern Politics and Government. London: Macmillan Press Ltd

Egbo, S. 2001. Political Soldiering: Africa's Men on Horse Back. Enugu: John Jacobs Classic Publishers Ltd.

Finer, S.E. 1988. The Man on Horseback. Bourdr. Co: Westview Press

Fourney, D. 1977. Congress and the Budgetary Process: The Politics of Military Appropriations. In J. Brigham, ed. Making Public Policy (65-137). Massachusetts: D.C. Health and Company

Halprin, M.H. 1975. The President and Military. In N.C. Thomas, ed. The Presidency in Contemporary Context (277-289). New York: Dodd, Mead and Company

Igwe, O. 2005. Politics and Globe Dictionary. Aba: Eagle Publishers

Jenkins, T.C. and Kposowa, A.S. 1992. The Political Origins of African Military Coups. International Studies Quarterly, 36: 271-292

Nnoli, O. 2003. Introduction to Politics. Enugu: Snaap Press Ltd

Obama, B. 2009. Obama in Ghana. <http://www.usaraf.army.mil>. Consulted 15 October 2013

www.ingramcontent.com/pod-product-compliance
Lightning Source LLC
LaVergne TN
LVHW021716060526
838200LV00050B/2692